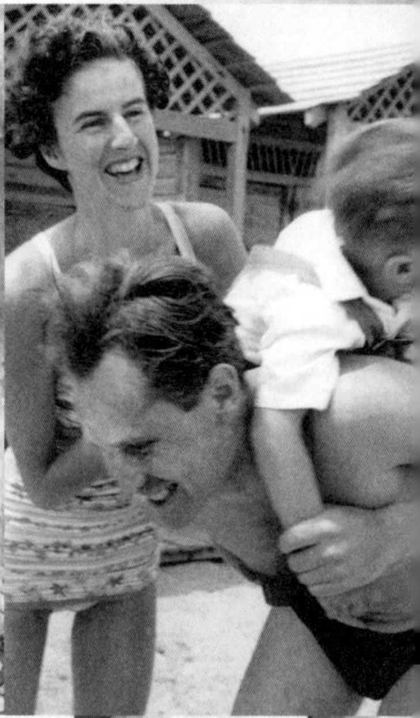

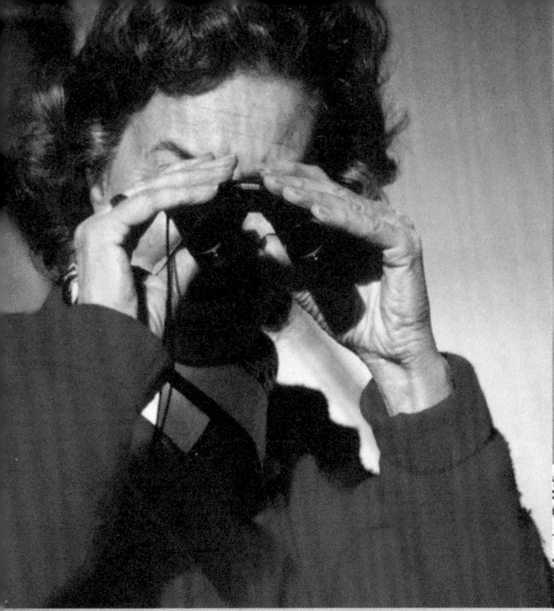

Texts by Sherin Kneifl

MATTEO THUN STORIES

CALLWEY

Matteo Thun nurtures an architecture and design practice that strives to create respectful and long-lasting solutions through a future-oriented lens. Born in South Tyrol in 1952, he was a student at the Salzburg Academy before completing his architecture studies in Florence. His formative professional years were spent under the guardianship of Ettore Sottsass—together, they co-founded the globally renowned Memphis Group in 1981. Several years a professor in ceramic design at the Vienna University of Applied Arts and creator of era-defining pieces, Matteo founded his eponymous architecture and design studio in 1984, where he would establish himself as one of his generation's most influential voices and talents.

STORIES

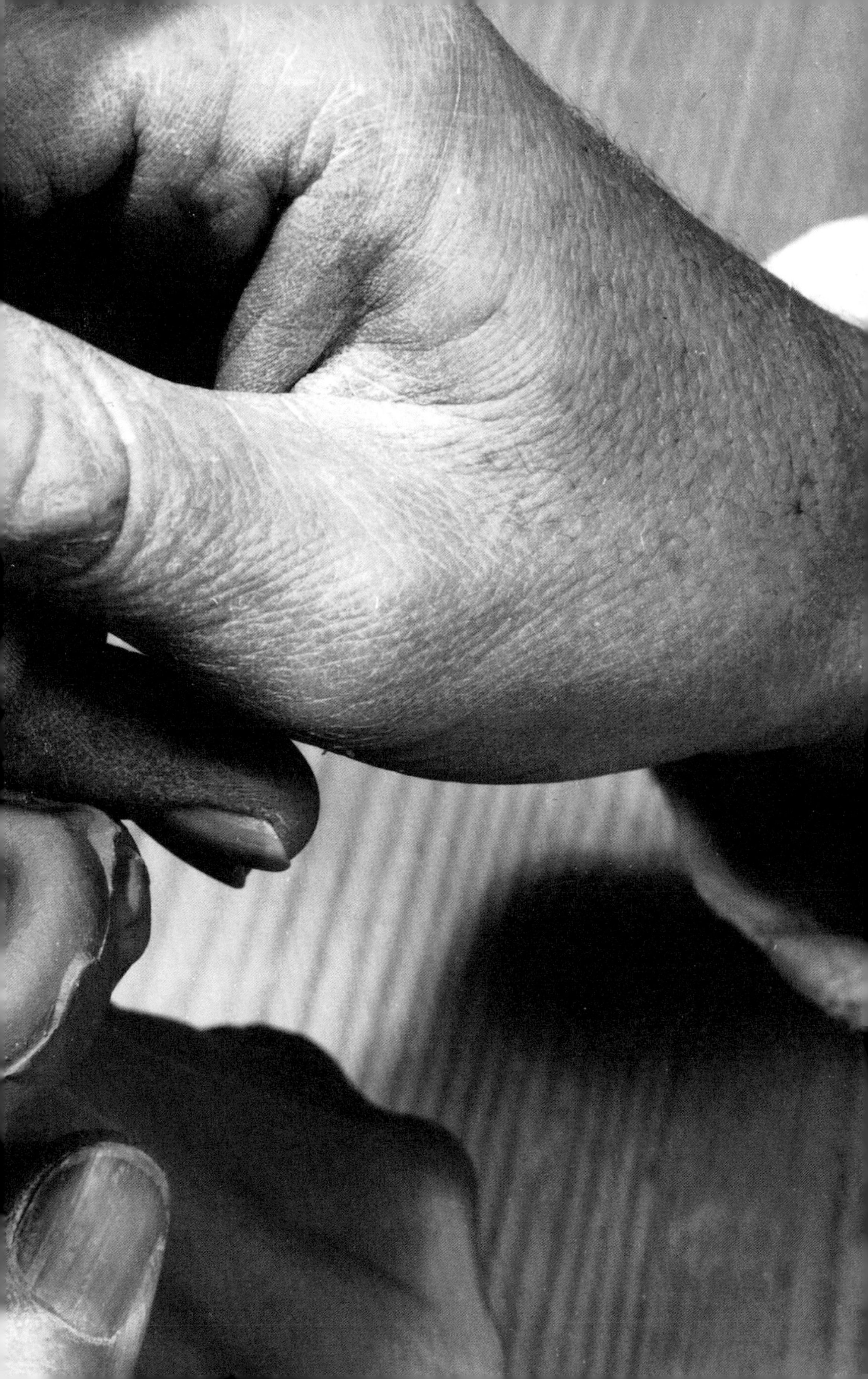

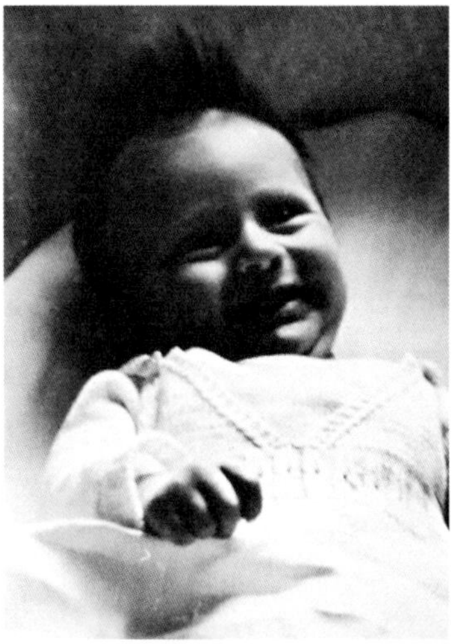

Lena Thun, Matteo Thun, Peter Thun

THE ANGEL OF BOLZANO / BOLZANO, 1952

It all began with an angel, the *Angioletto di Bolzano*. The heavenly figure marked the debut of Thun Ceramics, the pet project of my parents, who following their marriage felt inspired to create something together. Both had a penchant for craftmanship. My father, Othmar, Count von Thun und Hohenstein, held a doctorate in law but had also attended a ceramics school in Urbino shortly after the Second World War. My mother, Helene, was an Architect, always tinkering, painting or modelling. In 1950 they set up their ceramics workshop in the basement of our home, Klebenstein Castle in Bolzano.

The first angel appeared in the hands of «Lene» following the birth of her two sons, me in 1952 and my brother Peter three years later. Story has it that she modelled the angel after our sleeping image, with a chubby face, eyes closed, lips pursed, head slightly tilted back.

The idea of making angels was not a foregone conclusion. Although our family was of Catholic descent, I do not remember messengers of God being particularly welcome in our household. Personally, I never felt a profound connection with angels. In my eyes, the *Angioletto* is a symbolic mixture of South Tyrolean folklore and kitsch but, I have to admit that Lene had the right intuition—it was an instant success, the angel struck a chord with countless people and sold en masse.

As time passed, Thun Ceramics flourished, employing forty craftsmen. I was introduced as a small boy to help my mother check the quality of each angel figurine. By the time I reached seven I had become a diligent worker and was admitted to the production line.

The most important element was the face. For purely productive reasons the eyes *had* to be closed: open eyes are tricky, the pupils are so small. We would trace the two eyelids and accentuate the two dotted nostrils with a pointy stick, then form the singing mouth with a rounded one. The craftsmen were paid by the number of angels they produced. The faster you were, the more you earned. I worked hard on getting up to speed with them and by the time I was eleven, I had caught up with these professionals, even setting production records of which I was very proud.

The angel became the symbol of Thun Keramik. It still features prominently on wedding lists: «No wedding without Thun,» they say in southern Italy. My mother's ingenious creation brought financial security to our family.

Eventually, the manual production became unsustainable and the manufacturing was moved from South Tyrol to reduce costs and keep the selling price in line. My brother and I parted ways due to diverging interests and he left for China to run the company, which now manufactures in Vietnam and employs a few thousand people. **I observed with some regret the angel becoming outshined by all sorts of other figures.** But one thing remains the same: the angel still comes out of a plaster mould.

CLAY TOYS / BOLZANO, 1956–1962

As a child who made all his toys out of clay, I was delighted when, at the age of four, I discovered that I could make a turtle by simply pressing wet earth into the palm of my hand and adding five limbs. I soon mastered the process and the clay turtles became my first companions. In those days there were few toys to buy and they were very expensive, too expensive for my parents. Once I had produced a whole family of turtles, at the age of seven I tried my hand at making horse figurines.

Horses were a more challenging task as they stood on four legs rather than lying prostrate on the ground. Hours were spent concentrating on sculpting their bodies and manes down to the smallest detail. Gradually my manual skills improved and the figurines reached a satisfactory level of quality.

The Thun angel is the origin of my relationship with ceramics, a love story that I have never given up on. The love of manual work that my mother passed on to me and that I developed through play has stayed with me all my life. I stand out as the only one without a computer in my architecture and design practice. In the words of Italo Calvino, I strive for a more synthetic, faster and more precise approach, and my way is with pencils and watercolours. Essentially, I believe in the «intelligence of the hands.» I believe they guide the mind, not the other way around. For me, design is first about understanding what the hands are doing, and then the brain gives its approval. Or not.

Turtle made of clay

MÄRKLIN RAILWAY / BOLZANO, 1963

My Märklin railway was a labour of love and took up the whole of my playroom. The correct way to build it would have been to fix the tracks to a board, but I chose to leave the parts loose so that I could lay them as I pleased and have the trains run up and down the furniture. I also built two spectacular plaster mountains, one with a tunnel, the other with a swimming pool and even a trampoline. **Armed with patience, I glued whole forests onto them, one tree at a time.**

Before I had any tracks or locomotives, I saw a rerailer in a toy shop under the old arcades downtown. The curved metal device was designed to place derailed trains back on the tracks. My grandmother bought it for me, regardless of the limited use I could make of it. In anger or jealousy, my brother stomped on it and that was the end of the rerailer.

I ended up selling my whole collection—tracks, locomotives, carriages, wagons, signals, figures, the trees—everything. I made 60,000 lire, which I reinvested in a radio-controlled aeroplane. Its first landing was a crash and I lost my train, my plane and my investment.

A passion for flying since time immemorial

WOOD / BOLZANO, 1956–2024

The foundations of my career may well have been laid when I was four, when Uncle Roderick, my father's older brother, gave me a set of wooden building blocks. He was the founder of «spiel gut,» the organisation that still awards the best educational toys in Germany with its orange seal with a white dot in the middle.

I arranged the wooden blocks into sturdy, thick-walled houses. Some of their roofs were flat, others were gabled. What I liked the most about them was that they were I found them all beautiful, regardless of style. My parents were supportive and we would comment together on the quality of my buildings. Since she was an architect, my mother's praise was particularly motivating.

Building a house is one of our most primary instincts. All children like to play at drawing their dream home. We all desire to own a house, sleep in it, live in it, raise our families in it. This may be why there are so many detached houses, I suppose. I have felt this desire from an early age.

Our home was Klebenstein Castle. It is still there, at the end of Bolzano's Talfer river promenade, standing like a gateway to the Sarntal Valley. Only a few rooms were heated and I wasn't allowed to play on the stone-cold floor, so I would build my houses on one of the carpets lying around. The ceilings were wonderfully high, and I imagined the rooms of my wooden houses to be just as tall. Unsurprisingly, I don't feel comfortable in rooms with low ceilings, however cosy they may be. Length, width and height all affect our sense of wellbeing. The proportions of the castle have grown on me as much as I have grown in them.

It wasn't until many years later that I began studying Architecture. This complicated matters—statics, building technology, structural systems… all the fun and spontaneity was gone. My drawings were received with varying degrees of appreciation, some positive, others very critical. The notion of style gave me no rest.

I returned to the small scale, to product design. I found space to develop this with my role model and master, Ettore Sottsass, and his credo of holistic design, be it spoons or cities. The «Milan School» of combining design disciplines has stayed with me, as has the motto of looking to the future without nostalgia and designing with simplicity, lightness and durability in mind.

I have a renewed sense of these origins now that I am in my early seventies. I don't stack wooden blocks anymore, but I do build by piling up huge tree trunks with similarly simple construction techniques. The project that allowed me to return to this total simplicity is Jungle Hut. Here, there are no longer any questions of style, no space for discussions on whether minimalist architecture is beautiful or not. It pleases, and that is all. **When approaching total simplicity, questions of style become irrelevant.**

I seek reduction to the essential also in other aspects of life and this search for simplicity has proved more complex than seeking complexity itself. Just as Plato is easier to read than Heidegger, but possibly more difficult to grasp. I may be going against the tide, but for me wood is the building material of the 21st century. It is renewable, recyclable, has its own indoor climate and brings healthy insulation, including from noise. Like a sanctuary.

This is why I am now designing a place of self-discovery in the Alps, a gift to Jorge Bergoglio, better known as Pope Francis. All in wood, of course.

Wooden building blocks

Castel Thun in Nonstal

CASTEL THUN / NONSTAL, 1956–1966

Castel Thun, the family castle in the Non Valley, belonged to my great-aunt Teresina. Her son, uncle Zdenko, wasn't the most handsome of men, but by the age of sixteen he had earned a playboy reputation for being the first man in the valley to own a car. He used to race up the dusty roads to Castel Thun and the farmers would flee from the speeding car shouting, «Arriva il Conte! Arriva il Conte!» Gossip was spreading throughout the region.

When I entered my first year of primary school, Uncle Zdenko gave me this advice: **«You will manage with additions and subtractions. Next year, you will manage with multiplications. But keep away from divisions, you're never going to get it.»** His words still ring in my ears.

Aunt Teresina used to serve us children Campari Soda, for the simple reason that there was nothing else available in the castle kitchen. My mother tried to explain that children don't drink Campari, but she didn't care. Our time at Castel Thun was carefree, playing hide and seek or cops and robbers in the underground passages.

There were only two rooms in the castle that were heated in winter, yet there was an impressive collection of carriages, which were my uncle's passion. He even built a museum to house his collection, which still exists today. This expensive passion for carriages ruined him and he gradually lost all his possessions.

The tragedy of it all is that his mother had predicted that he would remain a bachelor, married only to the castle, but Uncle Zdenko eventually had to part with the castle too. He asked my father whether he wanted to buy it, but the roof needed repairing and that alone would have cost 64 million lire. My father had to invest the same amount in new premises for Thun Ceramics, so he did not go ahead and Castle Thun became the property of the State. It is now a museum.

THE WAY TO SCHOOL / BOLZANO, 1959–1963

My family lived in Klebenstein Castle, on the edge of the Sarntal Valley, on the banks of the Talvera River. From the imposing building, a riverside promenade divides Bolzano into the German-speaking old town and the Italian-speaking new town.

Although our house was on the German side of Bolzano and my brother and I went to the German school, we spoke Italian just as well. At that time, the German community tended to avoid the Italian community but there was no place for these cultural barriers in our circles, and friends from both communities mixed in our household.

With primary school came the first taste of independence, cycling to school. My younger brother pedalled diligently beside me, his little bike bravely navigating the promenade that led straight to school. **Along this short but eventful route we met a colourful cast of characters and embarked on our earliest adventures, which our youthful imaginations inflated and sometimes turned into terrifying nightmares.**

Like that fateful summer morning in 1960 when we saw a man sleeping on a bench along the promenade. Temptation set in and we approached him, stopped, and suddenly shouted into his ears. The man woke up in a startled panic and we made a hasty retreat, pedalling away at full speed. As the day wore on and our attention turned to lessons, the morning's escapade faded into the background. Finally, the school bell rang and we jumped back on our bikes. When we reached the promenade the man was still there, waiting for us, standing tall in his long black coat and ready to take his revenge. Miraculously, we avoided his grasp and narrowly escaped a severe beating, or worse, capture! For months Peter and I were terrified of ever seeing him again.

Our precious school breaks were often spent playing marbles or football in the square opposite. Goethe was an all-boys school and we were loud and boisterous. In the midst of this lively chaos, a stray football shattered a window of my great-uncle's residence, the Palais Toggenburg. The incident became a family affair and Peter and I had to make a formal apology to my uncle, the only living Prince Thun. He was in his eighties and rather unconcerned about the broken window, but he nodded approvingly as we bowed our heads in apology.

These are just a few of the many memories I made along the way before I enrolled in the Franciscan College. The Franciscan College may have been conveniently close, but it was worlds away from the joyful days of my first five years of schooling.

Matteo and Peter Thun cycling down the riverside promenade
Peter and Matteo

Matteo, second row, fourth from left, with his classmates and teachers at the Franciscan College

FRANCISCAN COLLEGE / BOLZANO, 1963–1964

I was extraordinarily unhappy at the Franciscan College. The brothers quickly understood that I simply did not like them and as I did not share their outlook on life, an inevitable path of misery lay ahead of me.

Greek was one of my few favourite subjects, I particularly liked the alphabet and the writing, not so much speaking or analysing it. My teacher, Father Ludwig, was as broad as he was tall and not at all on my side, and he would test me every Monday morning at 8:30, knowing full well that I knew nothing. Every week began with a public humiliation.

Father Hubert's size problem was even worse. His feet did not even fit into the Franciscan sandals usually worn by the fraternity, so he wore ladies' patent leather sandals instead. His role was to teach history but visibly this was not his mission, for his lessons were limited to us reading silently from our books. Occasionally he would ask a question, and one fateful day he addressed one to me. I mumbled incomprehensibly so he asked inquisitively: «What do you mean?» To which I replied, «Meinen tun die Hennen,» a German saying that roughly means «Hens do what they think»—which is, not much at all. Not a very considerate response, but it proved to be transformative. Brother Hubert immediately called the headmaster and, as one thing led to another, the day of the Councilium Abeundi arrived: I was expelled.

I was very happy to be exonerated from attending the Franciscan College, not so of the traumatic process, which is never easy to overcome as a child. After my expulsion, I was enrolled in the local state school, where I eventually got my diploma. This had not been my parents' first choice, but I like to think that I led the way for another fortunate outcome: my younger brother Peter went straight to state school, without the need for a Franciscan rite of passage.

THE SCHOOL OF VISION / SALZBURG, 1967–1970

I was so disappointed with school education that I asked my parents if I could spend my holidays doing something I really enjoyed. I had read that Oskar Kokoschka had founded an International Summer Academy of Fine Arts at the Hohensalzburg Fortress, the «School of Vision.» My parents agreed to send me.

Kokoschka's sessions lasted only twenty-five minutes and were very intense. The famous expressionist believed a portrait should be painted very quickly, looking at the model only briefly to weigh the proportions of the eyes, ears, nose, and mouth, and then complete the painting without gazing back. We were supposed to understand the person we were portraying almost instantly and, through sheer concentration, to capture abstractly their personality and, ultimately, their essence.

I was about fifteen years old and was sitting in the front row, a blink of an eye away from Mrs. Anneliese Rothenberger, our special guest model for the session. I tried very hard to capture her beauty in a wonderful portrait, but when it came to painting her eyes, in my rush and excitement I landed one of her pupils in the wrong place. The beautiful watercolour woman was no longer staring at me, one of her eyes had gone astray.

When the *Grand Master* took the revered soprano to admire the results, she stared in silence at my easel until he took her arm and said: «Come Madam, let's move on.» That marked the end of my career as an artist. I was the boy who had tried, and failed.

Kokoschka seemed to be particularly distracted by women that summer. Inge, his assistant, seemed to get much more attention than we did. So, I decided to travel upstairs in search of new opportunities, and I found Emilio Vedova.

He gave sensational lectures in the form of happenings. He was friends with Max Ernst, Salvador Dalí, Pablo Picasso, Henri Matisse, and exuded History of Arts. **We were now the speechless ones as Vedova danced around mimicking how Dalí painted, how Picasso drew:** «Now I will show you how Max Ernst would have done it.» With each of his sentences we became wiser, and in him I had found inspiration. I guess I came across Vedova only through my painful encounter with Anneliese Rothenberger. Perhaps my heart also led me there.

I still paint watercolours, but not as an artist. Somehow this path did not seem right to me. My sons see it differently, one is an artist, the other founded an art gallery. Kokoschka's immediacy in capturing proportions stayed with me. I always crystallise the vision for my architectures with watercolour on paper, it helps me define their proportion in relation to their context. As for Vedova, after having rejected the school system for so long, he became my master in how to make great things actually happen.

German opera singer Anneliese Rothenberger
Painter Oskar Kokoschka

Thun's Racer skateboard logo

MONTE MORELLO / FLORENCE, 1974

Legend has it that one of Leonardo Da Vinci's followers attempted to fly off Monte Ceceri in one of Leonardo's flying machines and the heavy linen wings soaked in beeswax caused a disastrous fall. In retrospect, it is fitting that my brother and I chose to test our Thun Racer on one of these Florence hills, Monte Morello.

Peter and I had discovered skateboards on a trip to California and, posing as young entrepreneurs, brought some back with the intention of producing our own and introducing them to Italy. We started producing the Thun Racer in Florence, where I was studying architecture. We would test the boards in the evenings and race them down to Sesto Fiorentino. One evening, in the dark and with no traffic around, I went downhill at full speed with a friend following me by car to light my way. It took a toad, lying still in the dark, to stop me and send me flying.

I knew I was bleeding from the chin, but I had no idea how badly I was hurt. We reached a bar to get a glass of water and recover from the shock. As I drank, water started dripping from my chin. The barista noticed and pointed to one of the customers, «This man is a doctor, you better go and talk to him before he leaves.» The doctor took me to his nearby surgery where he stitched up my chin without anaesthetic.

The Thun Racer was yet another way to satisfy my longing for speed. But this time I was left with a scar.

Nothing would work without my great aunts, a quintet of pretty sisters. Their father, the innkeeper of the Stiegl, believed that women should not marry, so from an early age each sister had her own role in the running of the family restaurant. They all remained unmarried, except for my grandmother, the black sheep among the six.

The clan was completed by three brothers, of whom I particularly remember Uncle Toni. His wife suffered from a fear of people and only went out after dark. From time to time I would meet her on the Oswald promenade, we would say a quick hello and continue on our way. Even relatives were too much contact for Aunt Hella. As a boy I sympathised with her, I understood well her fear of people.

Aunt Maria, the eldest of the sisters, was the one in charge. She counted Dora Mar among her friends, she frequented the Parisian scene and was on a first-name basis with Picasso, Max Ernst and many other artists. Endowed with a strong sense of style, she usually wore silk blouses with a foulard, her curly snow-white hair held up with a pin. Throughout her life she followed closely the latest works presented at the Venice Biennale, which she would comment on during our Saturday lunches. During one of them I tried my best to tell her about an artist, a certain Yves Klein, who painted only in blue, a special blue. She and her generation had little time for this sort of art.

Then came Great-aunt Nan, the pioneer. Not only was she one of the few women skiers in South Tyrol, but she would also drive around the mountains, with her lover in the passenger seat, for a few hours of indulgence.

After Nan came my great-aunts Pulla and Bab and my grandmother Rosi. The youngest of the sisters was called Carolina, but she was known as Pfiggele. Three generations of our family survived school only thanks to her. She taught Latin, Greek, mathematics and botany, and since my parents worked from dawn until dusk, she helped my brother and me with our homework, just as she had done with my mother two decades earlier and would go on to do with my brother's children twenty years later. She was extremely frugal and desired no possessions, her only craze was her Victoria, an amusing light blue German moped, on which she took us for rides. She never wore a coat, even in winter, instead sheltering from the wind by placing a newspaper across her chest. She saved five square metres of her garden for us to plant whatever we liked. My favourites were larkspurs, I really liked the blue of the flowers.

My great aunts not only laid the foundations of my life, they also nurtured my interest in art. These unusual women, each with her own interests, had gathered droves of artists around them, including Anton Faistauer, Albin Egger-Lienz and the Stolz brothers. Some of them, now famous and highly regarded, even painted portraits of the aunts. Lasting memories.

La Santa

FLYING / ALGHERO, 1974

I have a passion for flying and I have spent countless hours in the air. In my twenties I was particularly fond of free flying on a Rogallo, a simple and inexpensive wing that can be a kite, a glider or a plane depending on whether it is powered.

I would not be deterred from flying, regardless of the consequences. In 1974 I crash-landed on Lake Kaltern. A schoolboy mistake as I had attempted to land with a tailwind, which a pilot should never do. Taking off and landing should always happen against the wind.

My arm in a cast, I took my aircraft down to Alghero that summer. My objective was to launch from a cliff and make a spectacular sea landing in the blue waters of Sardinia. The large limestone rock inhabited by cormorants and seagulls lies just off the cliffs of Capo Caccia, a restricted military area. This made it particularly attractive.

I was granted permission by the Military Command to fulfill my ambition. After a few weightless turns I plunged into the sea and was pulled out of the water by my friends who were watching from a dinghy. The experience only lasted a few minutes and left me wanting for more. By the time we were back on land, we were determined to make a second attempt that same day, this time from the nightclub on the hill above Alghero.

I took off from the discotheque that evening, not unnoticed by the night crowd. A friend followed my flight path in his car. He claims to have stopped a shepherd from shooting down an unknown flying object: **«Don't shoot, that is a man!»**

← Free flying was my favourite thing

SUMMA CUM LAUDE / FLORENCE, 1975

While at the University of Florence, I had the privilege of working on the design of a bridge over the River Arno with Professor Leonardo Savioli. An accomplished architect known for his engaging lectures, Savioli had become a role model for me.

Unfortunately, Savioli's health deteriorated and he later was unable to supervise my thesis, so I turned to Professor Adolfo Natalini. In the sixties he had founded the avant-garde group Superstudio, which inaugurated the season of the Radical Architecture movement. Subversively, they claimed that architecture had no future.

Natalini invited me to his home to discuss the subject of my thesis. **«You do realise that it makes no sense to write a thesis on architecture, don't you?»** he said, and went on to ask me what I liked to do in life. I replied that I had a passion for flying. «Ok, then build a flying machine and present it. It's possible you'll get your doctorate with it. It might also get you expelled from the university. But that would not be so bad, architecture as a profession is dead anyway.»

That statement shook my world. I had wanted to study with Savioli because he had shown me a vision of creativity that was perhaps anachronistic, but very exciting. Savioli had designed monumental buildings and I dreamed of doing the same. Now I had to come to terms with the fact that Natalini was right, architecture in its classical sense had no longer any meaning.

Armed with his advice, I built a flying machine and presented it to the Chairmen of the Examination Board. The aicraft was suspended from the ceiling of the Brunelleschi Auditorium and I began the presentation showing a film of me flying it from Monte Morello. The soundtrack was «*The Dark Side of the Moon*» by Pink Floyd. It was all grandly provocative.

The experience took the board completely by surprise. They withdrew to deliberate and formulate their argument, which would supposedly conclude that architecture doesn't quite work like that. Among them was Giovanni Klaus König, a pioneer in aeronautical engineering. I later learned that he defended my work as serious and technically sound, and that he swayed the committee's opinion in my favour. Not only was the thesis accepted, but I was awarded the highest distinction, Summa cum Laude.

I now had a diploma certifying that I was an architect, but I began my professional career with little credibility, having defended a thesis that negated any future for architecture.

I made countless job applications and had just as many rejected, until I was offered a position with Richard Meyer in New York. My daily task was to operate a photocopier in the corridor leading to the toilets. The job was unpaid, but my reward was the freedom to take home copies of the drawings that most intrigued me to study them in detail, immersed in the hustle and bustle of that fascinating city that is New York.

Leonardo Savioli , Adolfo Natalini

CASTIGO DI DIO / NAPLES, 1976

I was 25 years old when I received the call to join the Military Service. As a university student I had been exempt, and I had hoped to escape this duty altogether. The Italian Authorities decided otherwise.

I was stationed in Salerno for two gruelling weeks, spending my time idly sitting in a truck or, worse, making rounds in the sweltering July heat. As a last resort, I tried to convince them that I was claustrophobic, only to be declared cured when they locked me in a small, dark room. My breakthrough, however, came when I staged an accident and was transferred to the military hospital in Naples.

The head doctor was favourably inclined towards me as he held South Tyroleans in high esteem for their renowned sense of honesty. He saw a chance for me: **«You have a year of military service ahead of you. If you would like to spend it here I'll train you,»** he offered, showing me around all the departments. Of course I accepted, anything was better than going back to Salerno, but I may not have lived up to his expectations of an ideal apprentice.

The Military Hospital was a former convent on the edge of the Quartieri Spagnoli, a notoriously crime-ridden neighbourhood where drug use was rife. I administered injections to about sixty patients a day and the nuns were responsible for handing me the drugs and the syringes. «We know very well that you sell them to drug addicts for a profit,» they regularly accused me when I came to collect them. I could not dissuade them and I earned the nickname «Castigo di Dio,» I was seen as God's punishment.

I was rather amused by my nickname so I began impersonating it. At night I slept in a dormitory, under the watchful eye of the Virgin Mary. In the dim light her sculpted figure appeared as if surrounded by a halo. She fell victim to one of my tricks when I bought a cheap strip of fairy lights and, much to the delight of the troops, the Madonna began flashing green, blue, red and yellow during the night. A nun marched in and asked who the sinner was. «It was God's punishment,» I replied with a clear conscience.

The medical knowledge I acquired during my time in Naples has been invaluable throughout my life. Nevertheless, it remains a glaring anomaly that an architect should provide medical treatment in a hospital. Little did I know that one day I would be designing hospital buildings and clinics. That year in the Military undoubtedly taught me what a healthcare facility should not be.

← Naple's Military Hospital

SUSANNE / ZERMATT, 1978

I first met Susanne, my future wife, in 1978. She was among the group of friends I had joined in Landquart to head for a skiing holiday in Zermatt. She paid little attention to me at the time. When we reached our stopover in The Valais, we had a lucky draw to see who would be roommates for the night and I got lucky, I was to share a spacious double room with Susanne. That evening, while we were both in our own beds, I started telling her stories. She seemed completely uninterested and eventually told me to be quiet. The following days we all had a wonderful time in Zermatt surrounded by winter snow. When we parted ways, Susanne remained on my mind.

We met again a few years later, when I contacted her after hearing that she had started a graphic design course in Milan. I have to admit that I had no clear strategy for convincing this remarkable girl to be with me. Instead of taking a romantic approach, I adopted a more carefree, «let's go» attitude and, surprisingly, it worked. Susanne did not seem used to this informality and was enjoying our time together. One day, during a stay in Voralberg, Susanne's village, we both felt that the stars had brought us together. **We were like two satellites whose orbits had aligned, and we decided to build a life together.**

We arranged to get married on the spur of the moment and it all happened very quickly. The village registrar had an unexpected opening the next day in his busy schedule as registrar, but also gas meter reader and graveyard attendant. We took the plunge and agreed that the civil ceremony would take place the following day. The challenge was to get hold of wedding rings, but a hardware store came to our rescue. Neither of us had anything fancy to wear, so Susanne opted for leather trousers and, instead of a veil, a floral wreath her mother crafted with daisies from the garden. When the time came, we lovingly slipped curtain rings on each other's finger, and said «I do.» I have great memories of our wedding day, the best was that I found someone who thought the whole scene was as romantic and funny as I did.

Susanne and I speak the same language and come from the same stable. We understand each other and, even after four decades together, our relationship is based on agreement rather than arguments. We share the same views and, for example, when we visit exhibitions we experience similar emotions without the need for explanations. Susanne has decorated all our houses. She has complete absolute creative freedom and I trust her completely. While I take care of technical aspects, the rest is her domain.

When Susanne and I worked tirelessly to establish our Milan practice agency, there was never any need to define our respective roles. Designs take two to three years to mature and reach the market, so you must anticipate future trends. Drawing on her fashion background and intuition, Susanne meticulously developed trend charts for each of our designs. She became the studio's radar.

For every product, from sunglasses to watches, Susanne created countless mood boards, to give clients a tangible presentation of the design direction. This approach was unique at the time, few went to such lengths, and it remains one of our strengths: our mood boards and material boxes speak volumes and our clients often find inspiration or identify the perfect sample, exclaiming, «Yes! That is exactly what I was looking for!»

Susanne Thun as a little girl
Susanne and Matteo: going through life together →

ETTORE SOTTSASS / MILAN, 1979

I met Ettore Sottsass by pure chance in Los Angeles and we shared a taxi to LAX airport. Back in Milan, I managed to get an invitation to visit him in his design studio, in via Manzoni 14, where I started working as a result my first job. There were only eight or ten people working there, some on typewriters and office equipment for Olivetti, others for his private clients. The studio was a hundred metres away from the Olivetti headquarters, where Sottsass gained his fame as a designer. We had access to their canteen for lunch, where we ate every day for 25 lire. We would then often make a pilgrimage to La Scala for a coffee that cost twice as much, but it was worth it to be in the same rooms once frequented by Maria Callas.

In Sottsass's studio I was assigned to design a collection of table accessories for Alessi. There had to be an oil and vinegar set, an ice bucket with ice fork and a breadbasket. Sottsass was adamant that they should all be stainless steel. He would give design instructions in the form of hand-drawn sketches on small pieces of paper. Their precision laid in the proportions, which had to be maintained intact.

At the time, however, a person was occupying Sottsass' thoughts. He was divorcing his wife of 27 years, Fernanda Pivano. She was a fierce feminist writer, fascinated by American literature, who had translated Hemingway, met Kerouac and Cassidy, lived through the rebellious years of the Beat Generation and, through her connections, had spearheaded Sottsass' career. When I was working on our Alessi deadline he hardly ever came into the office, and when he did he was not in the mood for small talk. **«You did not look closely enough. Look carefully at what I have drawn,»** was relentlessly his comment. I had to work alone and find my own way out without further clues, or the failure would be mine, and mine only.

Being left-handed did not help as I would inevitably smudge my drawings, earning comments from colleagues: «What are you doing, don't you know how a pencil works?» I had to learn by doing, and gradually I understood that I needed to start with a 7H hard lead pencil for precision, then switch to a 5H for definition, then finish with a soft HB to bring out the most significant lines.

Pencils are everywhere in my studio. Having sharpened and honed my skills working with Sottsass, I remain a firm believer in the creative power of hand-drawn sketches. Computers excel in many tasks, but, in my opinion, they are significantly slower at accurately capturing proportions.

Once a week, with my drawings in my briefcase, I would go to the Alessi headquarters in Omegna. The young Alberto Alessi would examine the drawings and generally agree with the designs, but his uncle Ettore, who was in charge of technical management, always thought they were too expensive. He had to be persuaded that a base was needed for both practical and aesthetic reasons as it would allow not only to carry oil, vinegar, salt and pepper together, but would also create the height necessary to elevate a simple table object into the essential element of a good table setting.

We fought a few battles but the set landed on their production line and, over forty years later, these designs are still a staple of restaurants and family dinners.

This was of course the creative achievement of Sottsass, but it made me very proud. There was nothing fashionable about the object, it was far removed from any design diktat. It was simply very useful and pleasant to place on a table. The proportions used in architecture did the rest, and the result will last forever.

Ettore Sottsass jr and Matteo

APEROL / MILAN, 1980

San Siro is the home of Milan's hippodrome and of the stadium of the city's two football teams, A.C. Milan and Inter Milan. I am not a football fan, but our family has supported Inter Milan ever since our cleaning lady gave Constantin a black and blue baby suit when he was born.

Instead of watching the games on television I had more of a bird's-eye view on them thanks to an agreement with Aperol: the orange drink from Padua entrusted me with flying their advertising over San Siro, exposing the brand to the crowds of the largest football stadium in Italy.

Every weekend we would take off with our Aperol branded wing from the «Montagnetta di San Siro» for our slice of the action, until a rival advertiser threatened to take us to Court to maintain their monopoly on flying advertising. They argued that we did not have an adequate licence, but everything was resolved thanks to a legal loophole surrounding the nature of our aircraft, which was neither registered nor recognised by the authorities. Thanks to this legal limbo, we were able to fly our banners not only over the San Siro and Turin stadiums, but also along the coast from Viareggio to Forte dei Marmi and between Rimini and Riccione.

We genuinely had a ball flying these banners.

Flying advertising

SIGNORINA RICCARDA / MILAN, 1979

Signorina Riccarda had the air of an old lady from a very young age, she spoke very loudly and no one ever doubted her chastity. There was always a very large bag hanging from the back of her chair, containing the key administrative files of the Ettore Sottsass studio. The reason for keeping the bag so close at hand can only be explained by the ease with which it could have been removed from the premises in case of a tax inspection.

My office overlooked the Coppola hair salon down in the courtyard. Rumour had it that ladies went there also to have their most intimate parts styled. Whether this was true or not I was never able to verify, despite the mirror on my desk. Signorina Riccarda often caught me carefully adjusting it. Another missed opportunity of mine in via Manzoni 14.

I lived nearby and used to cross the zoo gardens on my way to work. **Every morning my walk took me past a large cage of monkeys and after a while I developed a bond with them, I would even say a feeling of friendship.** They greeted me as soon as they saw me and I fed them some bread, under the illusion that they actually understood who I was.

There are other monkeys in our family chronicles. Vienna was once the home of my ancestor «Monkey Thun,» so called because he had monkeys as pets. He used to stroll around town with them on his shoulders. In those days, ladies wore elaborate hats, and the said Thun would send his little companions to inspect their fashionable millinery. He also carried a book on how monkeys walked, which he delighted in demonstrating on all fours.

Signorina Riccarda's ready-to-go bookkeeping

ANNA PIAGGI AND ANTONIO LOPEZ / MILAN, 1980

For decades, **Anna Piaggi was the most dazzling editor on the Italian fashion scene and Karl Lagerfeld's muse.** Lagerfeld's creative genius was particularly apparent in his collections for Maison Chloé, and Susanne and I were delighted when Anna Piaggi asked us to model some pieces of his winter collection. We were assured that Antonio Lopez would only take ten minutes to draw sketches of us wearing the clothes. The talented illustrator had been brought in to produce alternative spreads to the usual fashion shots.

The session took place in the studio of Anna Piaggi's husband, the black-and-white photographer Alfa Castaldi. Lopez sketched incredibly quickly and was blessed with an eye for the essential. But the session lasted two hours instead of the promised ten minutes, and the temperature in the studio rose and rose until I was on the verge of passing out in my winter cashmere tweed and fur.

Encounters with such luminaries changed my understanding of fashion. Susanne and I have attended fashion shows for many years. They influenced the way I dress only to an extent, but they are interesting indicators of the evolution of style in general. Susanne always points me to the designers to watch and the brands producing exceptional designs. All in all, it is a pleasure to take advantage of Milan's status as a fashion city.

I now only follow fashion shows digitally, but I never buy online because the instore shopping experience is essential, as I found out when designing boutiques in Milan, Paris and New York for Missoni, Fiorucci, Esprit and Hugo Boss.

Time changes you and what you choose to wear. At first I have been a fan of Gianni Versace's bespoke pieces. Then I turned to Canali, the understated elegance of Brioni and the timelessness of Hermès. Then I wore Prada for a long time. Now I prefer Loro Piana, especially in winter. As a rule, I buy pieces for life, not for a season.

Susanne and Matteo wearing the Chloé winter collection →

For Matteo & Susan
thank you for being so patient
wishing you the best – for everything x

SCIARA DEL FUOCO / STROMBOLI, 1980

Working with Sottsass was as rewarding as it was financially uncomfortable. The design rebel was a little relaxed about paying wages, and I was lucky to have other means of income thanks to flying advertisements.

In 1980 a friend and I were due to travel to Sardinia to run an advertising campaign and, armed with our two hang-gliders and our skis, we decided to make a side trip to the Sicilian island of Stromboli to fly over its volcano and ski down the Sciara del Fuoco, the lava trail that ends in the sea.

Once on the island, we painstakingly hauled our equipment to the top and took off over the strombolian eruptions and fumes. The gases and the sulphur were overwhelming, but we were ecstatic as we landed safely on the beach.

The next day, with skis slung over our shoulders, we climbed back up the side of the volcano and started descending the Sciara del Fuoco. At first we enjoyed a wonderful powder run on the very fine black volcanic dust that colours the island but, as we descended, the stones got bigger and our lungs filled with the dust. We had not planned for either of these issues, but we eventually reached the bottom, landing in the sea with our boots and skis. It is no longer possible to ski down the Sciara del Fuoco because a few years later a large chunk of the volcano subsided, causing a tsunami that affected a large area of the southern Mediterranean.

Entranced by our prowess we contacted Sports Illustrated, who bought our story and our pictures for eighty dollars. We had had the time of our lives, but the economic gain was disappointing. Back in Milan, Sottsass gave me an ultimatum: **«Make up your mind: either you fly and so you fly out of this practice, or you work with me and stop risking your life every weekend.»** After some consideration I promised to give up flying provided that we became partners. Sottsass Associati was born and at last I began to make a living.

← Skiing on the volcano
The photos of our adventure published in the magazine «Sports Illustrated» →

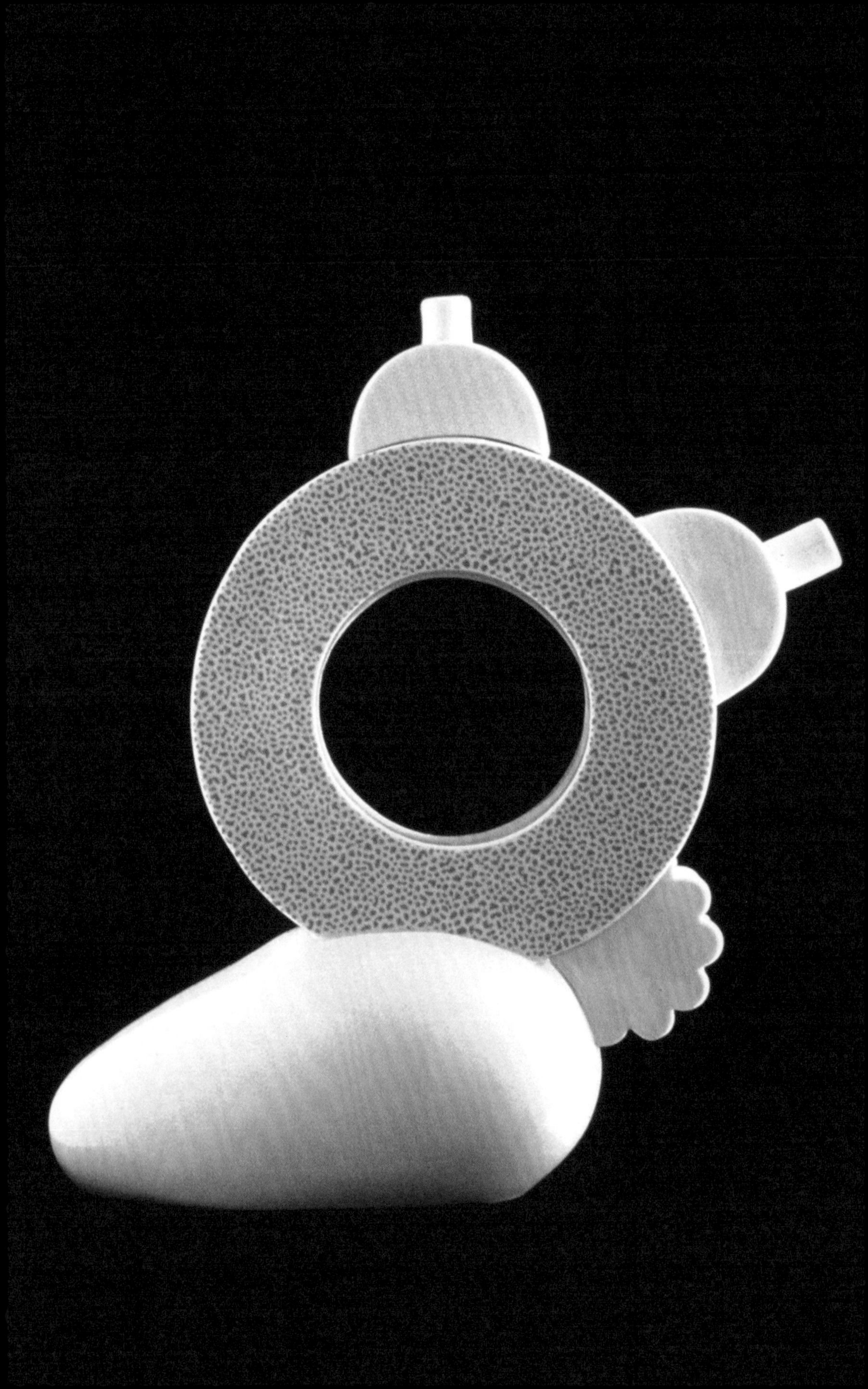

MEMPHIS / MILAN, 1981

I was working with the Florentine ceramist Alessio Sarri on a collection of coffee pots for Memphis, our design collective. I wanted to create a dozen coffee pots inspired by birds, recognisable by the different shapes of the lid, handle and spout. The origin of the «Rara Avis» collection of «rare birds.»

It was to be a limited edition of five and presented at the first Memphis event in Corso Europa, in the centre of Milan. For the opening day, Susanne had arranged to meet Alessio on the outskirts of the city to collect the birds and bring them to the gallery. The opening time arrived and there was still no sign of them. The press was waiting, and the road had to be closed because hundreds of curious people had gathered. Alessio arrived much later in the evening with the ceramics still hot from the kiln, having left Susanne to pace the dodgy suburban neighbourhood for hours.

The «Rara Avis» missed the launch, but **to our surprise, they became acclaimed pieces, bought by important museums, especially in the U.S., which exhibited them as pieces of modern art.** They received enormous interest from the press and the art world. I had never thought of them as works of art, nor had I expected the avian pots to find a home in museums. They were a semantic exercise, designed to test the limits of their material and of their function, but their primary raison d'être was to serve hot coffee. It is likely that they were never used for their original purpose as these rare birds turned out to be too precious to ever pour coffee in a cup, not even for me.

← Memphis ceramic pieces

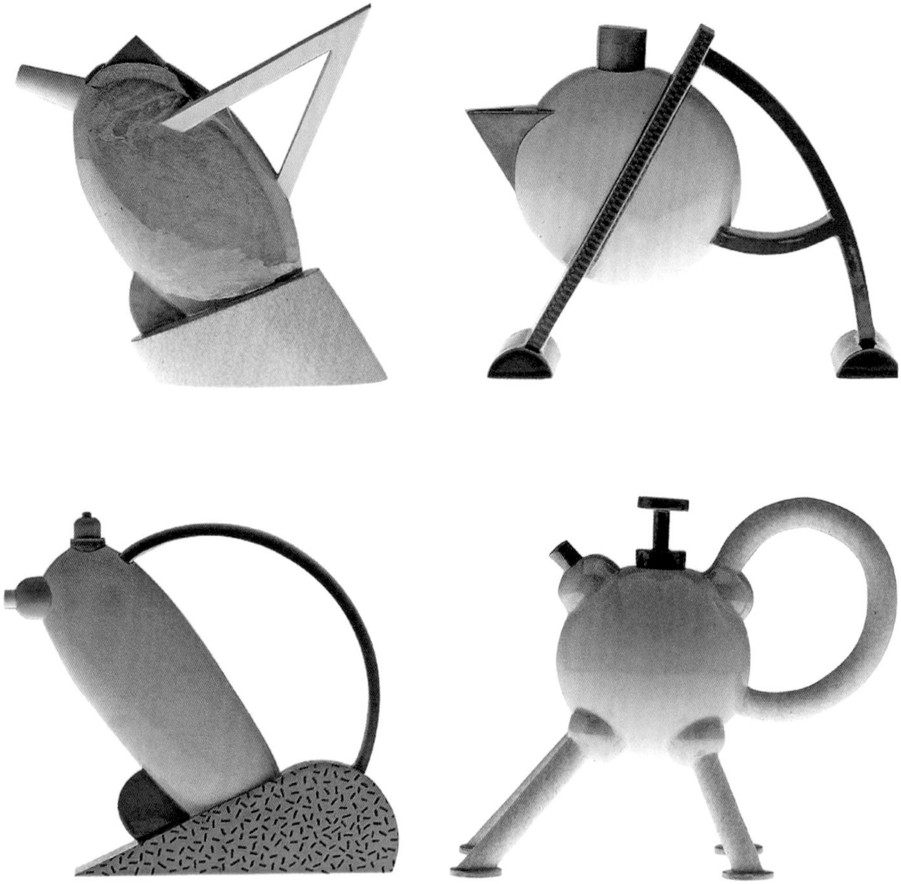

Rara Avis Collection, Memphis 1981

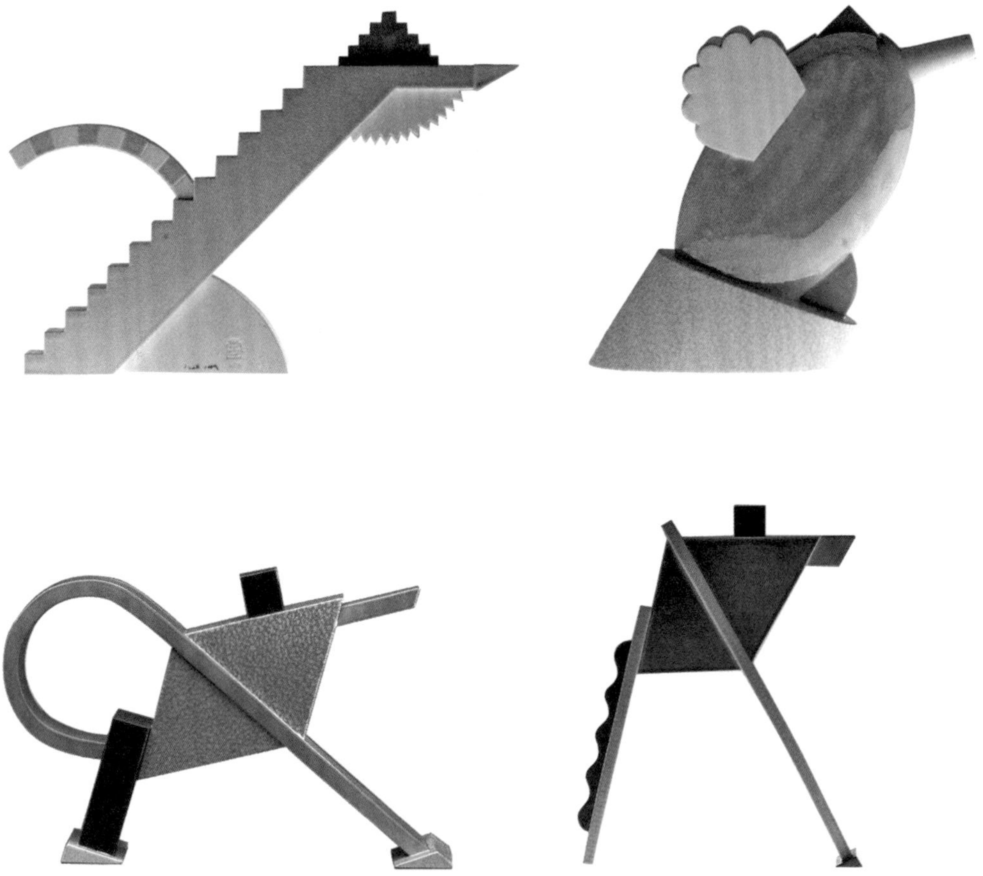

Rara Avis Collection, Memphis 1981

KARL LAGERFELD / MILAN, 1981

The day after the presentation of the first Memphis collection, which had caused such a stir, I received a phone call at Sottsass Associati. Apparently there was a German man in the showroom and I had to come straight away because no one could understand him. When I arrived I met this gentleman, who spoke very fast and in a conceited way. I eventually got his name, it was Karl Lagerfeld.

«Show me, show me, show me!» he said, so I took him round the exhibition. When we reached the exit, he ventured: «So, what should I do now?»—«Karl, why don't you buy it all!» I replied. He turned to his assistant and instructed: «Send everything to Monte Carlo,» then he left.

The Memphis group had been working without being commissioned, no one had asked us to design anything. With Ettore Sottsass, Andrea Branzi, Arata Isozaki, Michael Graves, Shiro Kuramata, Javier Mariscal, Nathalie du Pasquier, Hans Hollein and the others, we were just happy to be part of this unusual Milanese movement. We were expressing our frustration with the design industry, which had immersed us all in grey, purely functional and ergonomically driven objects. We felt the desire to break free, only design in the way we wanted and never expected to be paid for it.

Lagerfeld's wholesale purchase allowed Memphis to emerge from this limbo and establish itself. Obviously, the time was ripe to put a gloss on the «grey and ergonomically optimised» and our protest against functionalism spread like wildfire.

Fashion designer Karl Lagerfeld →

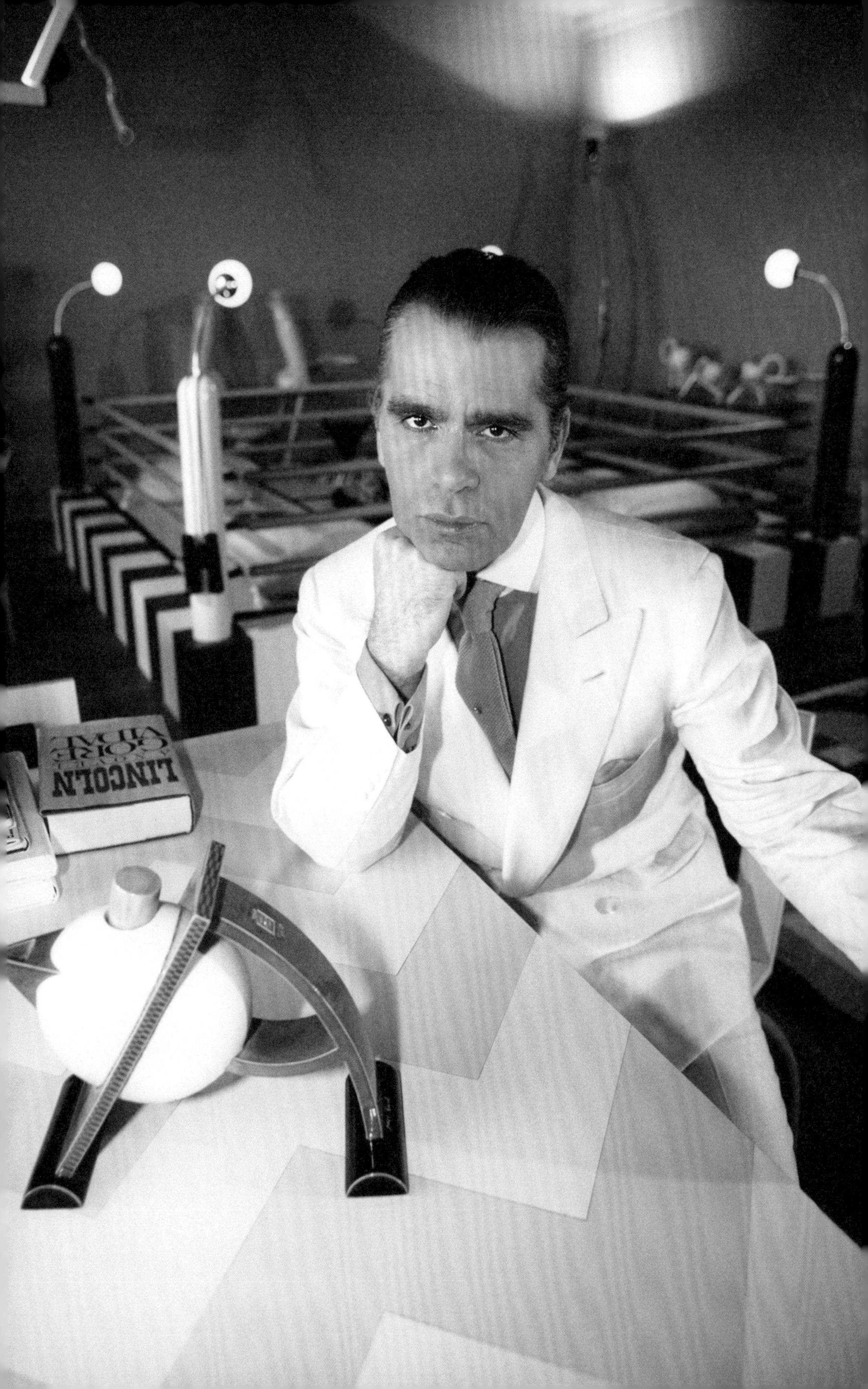
LINCOLN

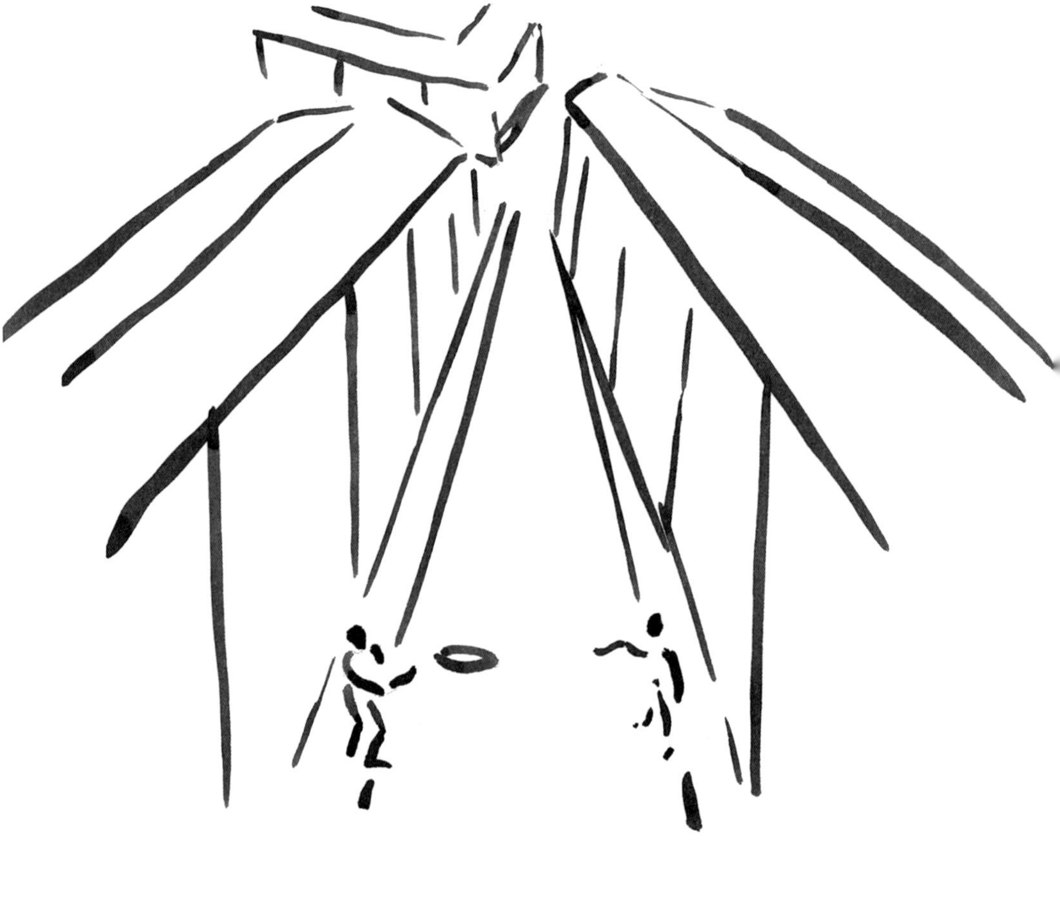

Playing frisbee in via Borgonuovo

VIA BORGONUOVO / MILAN, 1981

The first office of Sottsass Associati was located in Via Borgonuovo, a quiet street off Via Manzoni. The area was a magnet for creative people and became an inspiring environment where so many designers flourished.

We had managed to secure a basement, but we had no money for a secretary, so friends helped with the administration. It took an hour on average to produce an invoice in the middle of all the laughter.

Around the same time, Giorgio Armani set up his office across the street and at lunchtime we would play Frisbee with him and his friend Galeotti from either side of the kerb. When traffic was light we would venture to play on the road.

I never wore Armani's creations. I preferred Gianni Versace, he was fun as well as innovative. When we had our two children, Gianni had a bespoke children's collection and gave them both fabulous swimsuits made especially for them.

The world of fashion proved to be an important opening for our studio. We first designed a shop for the visionary Elio Fiorucci, a concept store that attracted swathes of new customers. Its success brought us to the attention of Esprit, which soon became our most important client. With the blessing of Douglas Tompkins, the company's founder, known to us as Doug, we had virtually free rein in expanding their store identity from Germany to rest of Europe. Only in our country did Esprit fail to pick up as a brand, the market remained dominated by the clothing giant Benetton, to whom the Italians were unmovably loyal.

VIA APPIANI / MILAN, 1984

On the hot morning of the 10 August, a tanned Ettore Sottsass, fresh from his stay in Bora Bora, appeared in the studio and I was greeted with a surprised «What are you doing here?»

I was sitting at my desk in Via Borgonuovo, to which I had been glued since the beginning of the summer, as you could see from my greenish complexion. I was trying to finish a presentation before everyone left for Ferragosto, the national summer holiday. But Ettore showed little interest in our new commission to design a control panel for Mandelli.

That day marked a turning point. I realised that my time at Sottsass Associati was over and that my place was elsewhere. I resigned. Only later did I find some consolation in the fact that the panel was rumoured to win the Compasso d'Oro, Italy's most prestigious industrial design award.

I found a place to set up my own agency in via Appiani, just around the corner from the infamous Ca' Brutta, Italian for «ugly house.» The building was designed by Giovanni Muzio in the early 1920s and is considered an example of early post-modernism. The lower part of the façade is in Renaissance style, while the upper floors are a mixture of styles. When it was completed, the large block of flats caused an uproar and the Milanese demanded that it be demolished. In my opinion, this was as crazy as Armani wanting to remove Aldo Rossi's monument to Sandro Pertini opposite his flagship store.

Ca' Brutta was finally redeemed in my eyes a year later, when Michael Graves, my American ex-colleague, came for the inauguration of my studio. Michael had become famous, among other things, for his Disney World Dolphin Hotel in Florida and had become a key figure in postmodernism. As we walked past the so-called monstrosity on Via Appiani, he stopped me in awe: «Matteo, someone has copied me!» he said in disbelief. I slipped in that it had been there since before he was born.

What he did not seem to realise was that the Italian Rationalists, of whom Muzio was a prominent representative, were forerunners of the Postmodernist movement. The Postmodernists had only recently made their debut at the first International Architecture Biennale in Venice in 1980. «Strada novissima, la presenza del passato» was their statement. By reintroducing the past on the creative map, their school of thought challenged the Modernists' future-driven perception of technology and geometric forms. They promoted a synchronic vision of history because they felt that the present didn't offer anything new. The movement waned within a few years, and no one talks about postmodernism anymore. I, for one, tend to be overwhelmed by the scale and opulence of their architecture.

Giovanni Muzio's Ca' Brutta

Professor at the Angewandte in Vienna

UNIVERSITY OF APPLIED ARTS / VIENNA, 1983–2000

I had just turned thirty when the University of Applied Arts in Vienna offered me a professorship in ceramics. I thought it would be a good idea to do it for two or three years, to give me some credibility as a young professional. I turned to Ettore Sottsass for advice and he strongly advised me not to do it: **«Don't waste your time teaching, concentrate on your designs,»** was his conclusion. He had never accepted a professorship, neither had Renzo Piano at the time.

Chance would have it that Lagerfeld had also been asked to teach at the University of Applied Arts. «Don't be silly, go once at the beginning of the course and then again at the end of the semester. Whatever you do in between, they can learn from the magazines they buy at the tobacconist on the Stubenring,» was his straightforward position. If Karl was going to accept the professorship, so was I.

At my inaugural lecture, the front row was occupied by other professors, all in their sixties and all waiting for this young man from Milan to start talking nonsense so they could send him home quickly. I presented ten specimens of the «Rara Avis» as my research project and introduced my intention to spend a few years teaching and experimenting with ceramics. The audience soon began to protest and boo. One student asked about my didactic approach. Unprepared for the question, I replied that I had no didactic principles. The booing intensified and my debut became very uncomfortable but I was awarded the professorship and even got a diplomatic passport.

But my colleagues' envy became a problem. I set up my masterclass at the Angewandte as a small factory, and every year I invited several industrial sponsors, first Alessi, then Rosenthal, then Villeroy & Boch, and so on. Representatives from these companies came to teach on very concrete business aspects, which was very useful for the students, but these sponsors also provided considerable funding for the course, which we spent on study trips to China and New York. These initiatives were fully privately funded, and this annoyed the academic authorities immensely. Given that my motto on these trips was «sleep all day and party all night,» the university should probably have handed my notice for being so careless, but I ended up leaving of my own accord.

Rara Avis, Red Collection, 1984 →

STUDIO OPENING / MILAN, 1984

In 1984 we were ready to open the via Appiani practice studio and this called for a celebration. The floor hadn't yet been laid yet, but nothing was going to stand in the way of a good party. «Architectural Attire» was the dress code and several hundred guests played along, turning up in inspired costumes. My parents were dressed as birdcages, Susanne as the Duomo of Milan. The eclectic crowd set the tone for the party, which kicked off in earnest with breakdance street performers we had recruited in Piazza del Duomo.

Spirits were high when my first customer came back through the door, pale as a ghost, his trousers torn. «You're lucky I'm still alive!» he said approaching me with his arms open wide for a hug. While dancing he had taken one too many steps backwards and fell out of the window. He was miraculously unharmed except for a few bruises, some scratches and a ruined suit. The party went on in full swing.

There were creatives from all walks of life, fashion designers, artists and architects. Everyone was happy and doing well, working on what they loved to do. We were at the centre of Milan's creative storm, ready to embrace the world. Nowadays it seems that seriousness, law and order always prevail. I miss the lightness of those days.

I had found my professional home and, forty years later, I still go there every day. Over time, the studio grew, first taking up new premises around the second courtyard of the building. Not only were we in an ideal location, just a few metres from Piazza della Repubblica and its underground, trams and taxis, but the layout, by gradually extending to other residential units, organically formed dedicated spaces for each department, where they can create and develop their own identity, whether they are Architects, interior designers, communication or administrative staff. We call it the Appiani family.

Some insular meeting rooms are devoted to brainstorming, and phones are not welcome. There is also our underground vault where our precious materials archive is kept, an intimate space where we assemble our material boxes to give clients their first taste of how their scheme will feel like. The soul of our home is the kitchen, where we get together every day around a plate of freshly cooked pasta.

The studio has also expanded to Munich, into fabulous spaces where our colleagues help us through the nine lives work phases of a German architectural project. They provide the valuable connection and dialogue we need to bring projects to a successful conclusion.

Back in Milan, we also have a studio on Corso Venezia where we develop our product designs. Working on small projects involves a different pace and logic; products come to market in two or three years instead of the average six it takes to complete a building. In product design, it is about capturing the soul of the brand and understanding the industry; in architecture, it is about capturing the soul of the place and understanding the wind, the sun, the landscape, the people. I am fortunate to feel at home in both.

The theme of the opening evening was architectural attire →
Susanne and Matteo at the studio opening party →

MILANO
I
NO

Keith Haring

KEITH HARING / MILAN, 1985

The *Latteria San Marco* is affectionately known as «da Maria,» after the owner who, with her husband of sixty years, Arturo, has been running for decades what I consider to be the best restaurant in Italy. Their small premises are not particularly attractive and can only seat thirty people, but the authentic zero-kilometre food that Arturo grows, buys and cooks every day with unwavering dedication and the cheerful atmosphere that prevails are more satisfying than any fancy interiors. The choice of wine is simple: it's either red or white.

How Arturo and Maria's place has managed to be so popular for so long is hard to explain. The food is so ordinary that many wonder what's so special about it, but it all boils down to the seasonality of their simple pasta dishes. It's spaghetti al *limone* when the lemons are ripe, replaced by spaghetti ai *spinaci* when the spinach harvest begins. That is all, and it is simply delicious. My personal favourite, whatever the season, is the bulgur with freshly cut vegetables.

To get a table, you have to be there by 12 noon sharp, and no later than half past seven for dinner. The place is packed within minutes, still customers continue to line up in the street waiting for a table. While Arturo cooks, Maria manages the service and the lady of the house inevitably knows everything about everyone. In a place where millionaires mingle with railway workers, she knows how to handle gossip with discretion.

Where else could I take Keith Haring? I had first met him in New York in an abandoned office building where a club had been set up, with a bathtub filled with ice for serving drinks and a DJ playing the latest sounds. I was soaking up the incredible atmosphere when we met, and he was accompanied by Blondie. The kind of night only the Big Apple could offer. Keith was now making frequent trips to Milan to visit a friend who ran another club and these visits were our opportunity to catch up.

In the lively atmosphere of the *Latteria* we dined on salad, pasta, fish and a large carafe of wine. When we finished, Keith picked up an empty plate of spaghetti from the table, grabbed a black felt-tip pen from his pocket and began to draw. In a minute, instead of traces of tomato sauce, the white porcelain was covered with one of his signature characters. Maria came over to clear the table and, unimpressed told me: **«Please tell that lunatic to stop messing with my plates.»** I suggested that she leave the plate untouched and put it in her safe. «If you say so, I will, but I don't see the point!» Today that plate is worth twenty thousand dollars.

A MANIFESTO ON THE SURFACE / VIENNA, 1985

The time was ripe for me to voice my manifesto, and in the true spirit of Memphis, it was to be disruptive. I wanted to experiment with applying the notions associated with small-scale design objects to large-scale architecture. Many of my peers only talked about architecture in terms of space and how it was experienced; the surface, the cladding, the way architecture was dressed seemed less important.

I set out to dress architecture in big clothes and started working on an exhibition of skyscrapers in a «heavy dress» that told the story of what happened inside and why the buildings were there in the first place. Peter Noever, the director of the MAK, the Museum of Applied Arts in Vienna, agreed to host the exhibition. Gottfried Semper's buildings stand out dramatically on Vienna's main thoroughfare. He was a master of architectural cladding, so it is more of a shell than a space.

There was a snowstorm on the night of the opening, and as I got out of the taxi I looked up and smiled: the banner over the entrance read «A Manifesto on the Surface,» and it fit the exhibition like a glove. I shook Peter's hand warmly, grateful for the pun. A crowd had gathered long before the doors opened at 9 p.m. and the architectural establishment soon gave their verdict and ridiculed the exhibition. One of them, Hans Hollein, was determined to make his voice heard, but thankfully Peter did not hand him the microphone.

The controversial collection of «heavily dressed» headquarters included one for the International Olympic Committee, featuring all the Olympic sports, and a «United Vatican,» a large obelisk in the centre of St Peter's Square around which all the world's religions could sit, unthinkable in the eighties. Others included an architectural impersonation of the World Bank in downtown New York and a United Airlines building in the form of a unified terminal at JFK airport. An international hotel chain was also given a heavy outfit.

The happening received the expected amount of criticism, but I was pleased with its success: the «Heavy Dress Exhibition: Manifest of Architecture» went on tour to Chicago, the birthplace of skyscrapers, and then to Frankfurt, Europe's high-rise capital.

The inaugural Heavy Dress Exhibition at the MAK in Vienna →
The exhibition travelled from Vienna to Chicago →

CAMPARI / MILANO, 1985–1990

I have been lucky to work with interesting clients from early on, but one of them was a legend: Campari. The headquarters of the iconic Italian red bitter brand were located on the street parallel to Via Appiani, only a stone's throw from the studio. Their offices could be described as a temple of elegance, with a style that would turn any visitor into a fanatic.

Davide Campari inherited his father's artisanal liqueur-making business and turned his name into a brand. Then, Domenico Garavoglia took over and transformed the company into the international success story we know today. Rosa, his wife, shone with nobility and dignity and was always surrounded by five assistants, all of them purely decorative and completely useless in facilitating my business relations with her. At the time, Rosa wanted new designs of Campari glasses, a whole range of branded Christmas gifts and VIP give-aways, bar clocks, ashtrays and, my favourite, a «*rendi resto,*» a swinging small change dispenser.

Every month I had a session with the Signora to present new designs, which were mostly inspired by the works of Fortunato Depero, the exponent of Italian Futurism. Depero had created countless groundbreaking advertisements for Campari at a time when no one believed in advertising as an art form. His eye-catching images and progressive approach to PR proved to be my salvation: no matter how daring my designs, Mrs. Garavoglia had no choice but to embrace his legacy and pretend to be progressive too.

Depero's iconic «Spiritello» character helped me to create my most memorable Campari object, the cocktail shaker. The stylised «Spiritello» was featured in advertisements jumping, dancing and generally enjoying drinking Campari in extravagant V-shaped glasses. During my research I had came across the Boston Shaker, the simple combination of a glass and a metal tin used on the luxury cruise liners of the Belle Époque to mix large numbers of cocktails. Together with another client, Alessi, we created the new Campari Boston-style shaker by applying on Spiritello's conical glass a metal lid in the shape of his hat.

The Campari Group is now an international drinks giant that owns the French orange liqueur Grand Marnier, as well as Aperol, Cinzano, Cynar, Frangelico... But it is still the red bitter from Milan that epitomises the Italian way of life. The Campari Spritz's place at the top of the *aperitivi* list has only recently been challenged by the Negroni cocktail, which still requires 40ml of Campari, whether made the proper way or the Sbagliato way. *Salute*!

← Alessi Shaker
Via col Vento glass, Lobmeyr Vienna →

VORWERK / HAMELN, 1988

I am used to receiving briefs and I generally prefer to get clear instructions with accurate definitions. But, no matter how clear a client's ideas are, dialogue remains essential. In every project there comes a breaking point when mental flexibility is needed on both sides to overcome differences of opinion and take a project to the next level. One that could not have been foreseen.

I was contacted by Vorwerk to contribute to their Dialog Art Collection exhibition of carpets by artists and architects. I was basically told to do what I wanted, a non-briefing for a piece that would sit alongside those of Peter Behrens, Gottfried Bohm, Norman Foster, David Hockney, Roy Lichtenstein and Jean Nouvel. Finding myself in this creative mix of peers and artists caused me a certain amount of uncertainty, as it often does.

Is an architect a building artist or a building engineer? This ambivalence remains unresolved. Brunelleschi, the master builder of the dome of Santa Maria del Fiore in Florence, resolved this dilemma by creating a masterpiece in which the distinction between art, craft and architecture no longer mattered. In general, however, architects don't experience the same level of freedom enjoyed by artists. What architects do is determined by the soul of the place, the climate, the culture, the dialogue with the client, the legal and structural requirements, as well as creativity. We have to work with these restrictions, which can also be seen as opportunities, depending on how you approach them.

For the Vorwerk collection I wanted to create a piece of art that would give energy to a room, like a power pack that would have to be replaced periodically because its visual impact would inevitably fade over time. I presented two, a red and pink leopard pattern and a Memphis-style infinity pattern that had no beginning, no end and no rhythm.

It was a real pleasure to curate the first exhibition of the collection at the Deichtorhallen in Hamburg. We presented the carpets hanging on the walls, like large canvases. The exhibition resonated around the world: a utilitarian, oversized surface was transformed into an energising element of interiors.

Carpet design by Matteo Thun →

illy

ILLY / TRIEST, 1990

Although people can have different tastes, Illy was once considered to be the best espresso by coffee connoisseurs. Ernesto Illy had the simple but ingenious idea of not roasting blends of coffee beans, but only the finest Arabica beans, so under his guidance there were no blends at all. A food chemist, Ernesto wanted his coffee to be drunk from a cup that would preserve all of its aroma, so he produced sixty pages on what he thought the best espresso cup of all time should be.

I received this impressive briefing at the company's headquarters in Trieste and I congratulated him on his detailed vision of «*the best espresso cup*.» What a challenge! The superlative in that sentence gave me pause, but if ever there was a design I needed to master, this was it.

A year later, I returned to Trieste with a plaster mould prototype of the cup. Recognising the importance of how a cup feels on the lips, I had refined the upper rim to make it thinner, while retaining a thicker base for the «*fornello*» effect, which ensures that the espresso flowing into the cup maintains a temperature above eighty-five degrees. The resulting cup looked deceptively simple—a rounded porcelain cup with a circular handle—but its technical features were studied meticulously.

While the shape of the white porcelain cup was approved, there was contention over its lack of «dress.» Traditionally, branded coffee cups were promotional items, not for sale. I suggested an alternative marketing strategy: inviting artists to decorate the cup instead of using the Illy name. This creative idea was initially met with scepticism, but after a few weeks I was instructed, «Find five artists; let's give it a try.»

What started as an experiment with local artists blossomed into an art collection. **Today, these limited-edition cups are sought-after collector's items, with over five hundred designs. The cup is the brand.** The name needs no mention for it to be recognised as «the Illy cup.»

I seized the chance to design my own editions for the Illy Art Collection, drawing inspiration from the sensations brought by drinking an espresso: it's hot, it invigorates the senses, it's consumed in a moment, it's economical, and it's a universal daily ritual. Illy recruited an art director from Cologne, dedicated to selecting international artists. Each artist, from Jeff Koons to Francesco Clemente, James Rosenquist, or Ron Arad, is paid a symbolic fee of one thousand euros to showcase their creations on «the world's smallest canvas.»

← Illy espresso cup
Illy Nude espresso cup →

TIFFANY & CO. / VENICE, 1990

Venice would not quite be Venice without Harry's Bar, the place where all Venetian tales meet, some steeped in truth, others veiled in myth. The birthplace of the Bellini, a simple concoction of prosecco and white peach puree, maintains an irresistible charm and is guaranteed to offer both good company and a vibrant atmosphere.

One evening, after a few drinks, I decided to head back. As I was leaving, a gentleman approached me and, in the usual casual American way, asked me how I was and where I was from. His name was John. Our conversation picked up and we walked together for some distance until we reached the Accademia Bridge and he challenged me: **«Let's walk on the railing, let's see if either of us can cross without falling into the water.»** On the spur of the moment and feeling confident, I accepted; I was after all a good swimmer and the balancing act on the 25-centimetre-wide railing didn't seem too daunting. We both made it dry to the other side and this innocent game marked the beginning of a lasting friendship.

John Loring was Design Director at Tiffany & Co., so he extended an invitation to visit the company in New York. Curious and intrigued, I was ceremoniously welcomed into the jeweller's prestigious hall. Our discussions soon turned to my potential contribution to their home collection.

John was passionate about Murano glass, so we arranged to meet again in Venice, this time on the island of the glassblowers. There he introduced me to Archimede Seguso, perhaps the most eminent master glassblower of his time, who personally produced all the prototypes for Loring. Seguso took out a few pages of newspaper and a black chalk and asked me to draw what I had in mind. I sketched a vase decorated with three Greek graces, Seguso's hands transformed them into glass. My first contribution to Tiffany & Co. was born.

Other designs followed, including the Rinascimento collection, a series of geometric blue crystal vases reminiscent of delicate sculptures, and a desk clock. Working with Tiffany's helped me understand the workings of these coveted and globally distributed brands. The experience reinforced my belief that while marketing, distribution, and financial factors are all important, the product itself is paramount. Above all, the product must be exceptional, even when presented in an iconic turquoise gift box.

Working with John Loring also taught me another invaluable lesson: chance encounters and spontaneity lead to great things. Who would have thought that a carefree evening in Venice would give rise to all this?

Matteo with his Tiffany & Co. collection →

I had already designed a few watches, namely for Bulgari, when the Art Director of Swatch asked to meet me. It was my experience in the Memphis Group that they were interested in; they felt that this would give me the right perspective on the disruption that Swatch was causing in the watch industry. That much was true, I do have an affinity with disruption.

I took the job and set up a Swatch Lab in Milan with a team of international graphic designers, tasked with creating two collections of 62 watches a year: 124 models went into production each year. Meetings with representatives of the various markets were always a challenge, as they all had their own ideas about the models that should be included in the collections. The Americans, for example, wanted «a white watch with white figures, nothing but white, because we have several million doctors and white is their colour.» The French wanted something completely different, as did the Italians. But we all shared a common denominator: the material had to be plastic.

The disruptive production process imploded when the CEO, Ernst Thomke, told me categorically: **«I need a metal Swatch.»** «OK,» I replied, «how much can it cost?» He gave me a utopian figure and left the room. I was certain it would not work. It had to look like a Swatch and be just as affordable, which was famously achieved by reducing the clock movement to only 110 parts. Nevertheless, I discussed it with the experts at Eta's Grenchen factory—and they all shook their heads.

Months went by before I could present the CEO with a metal Swatch, meticulously designed to minimize production costs. Upon hearing the cost, he nearly flung the watch at me. Stunned, I insisted that I needed his help to make this work. Reluctantly, he referred me to another manufacturer in Grenchen, whom I contacted immediately. These specialists had pioneered a sintering process, enabling the creation of metal objects by bonding metal powders. This innovative method was our lifeline, allowing us to produce the metal Swatch at the desired cost. The «Irony» model became the first non-plastic Swatch and remains a timeless classic.

For several years, I also oversaw the brand's in-store displays, but most jewellers showed little interest in stocking our affordable, colourful watches. The profit margins were too slim, and the recurring refrain was, «When we sell a Swatch, we earn a fraction of what we would get with a Rolex.» As a result, we decided to develop our own concept stores.

← Swatch clockwork in its plastic case
Christmas special by Matteo Thun →

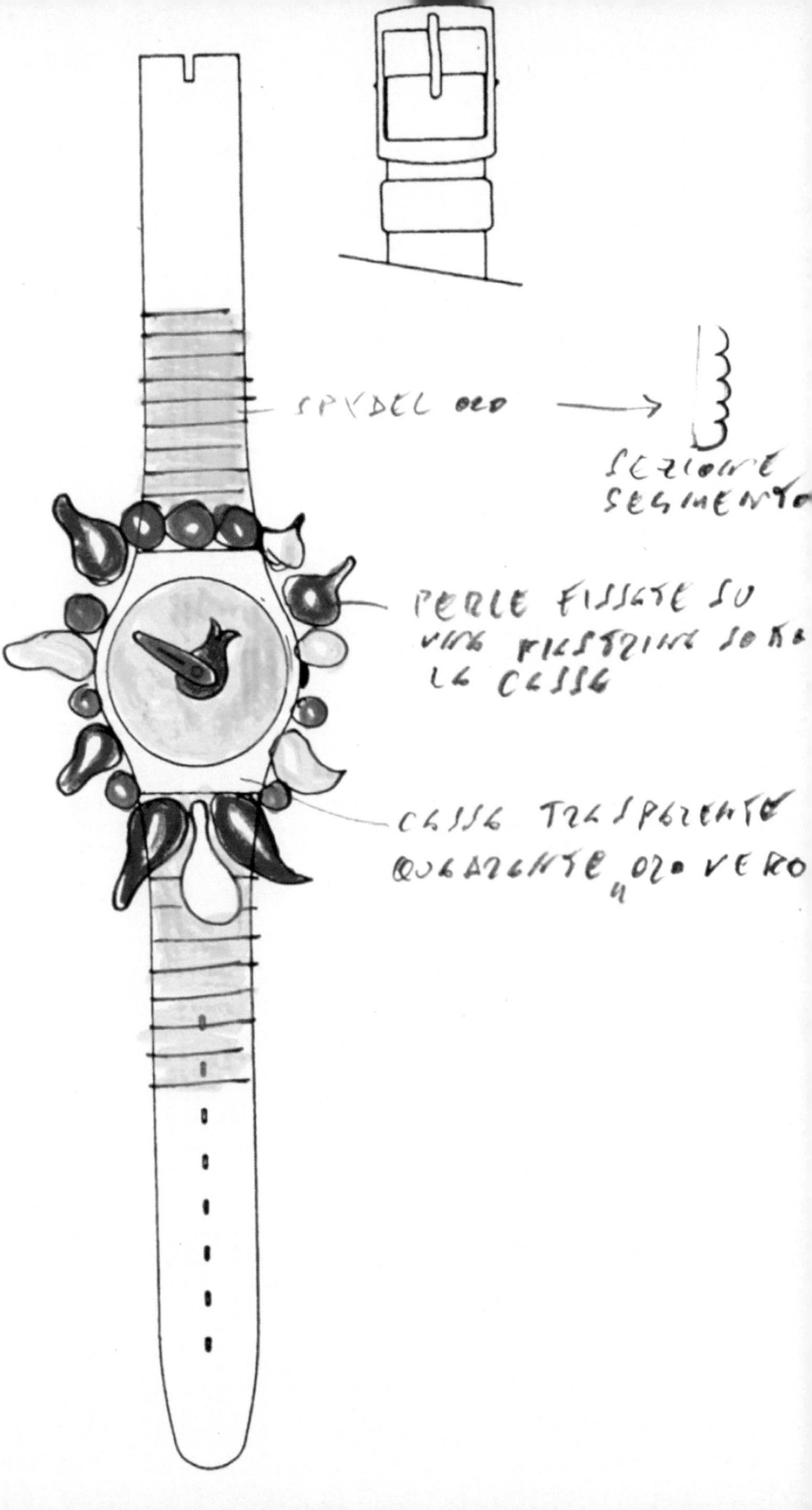
SPIDEL ORO
SEZIONE SEGMENTO
PERLE FISSATE SU UNA PIASTRINA SOTTO LA CASSA
CASSA TRASPARENTE
QUADRANTE ORO VERO

Engadin Postcard

OUR SECOND HOME / ENGADINE, 1990–2024

In 1990 Susanne became pregnant and our second son was due—of all days—on Christmas Day. Traditionally, we went skiing for Christmas, so we were keen to try and make it work all the same. Susanne asked around and found that there was a very well-regarded gynaecologist in Samedan. When she contacted him, the doctor was quick to tell her that he was unavailable until the spring, but Susanne was not about to let him go and exclaimed, «But my due date is in December!» «All right, come and see me and we'll see what we can do.» Within minutes, she had him wrapped around her finger, and they both got on very well. We were delighted to be in good hands for the birth, and we went ahead with our plans, renting a house in Celerina.

The doctor turned out to be a real blessing, giving Susanne a sense of confidence that she hadn't experienced in Milan four years earlier, in the run-up to the birth of our first son, Constantin. When Susanne went into labour and was admitted to the hospital in Samedan, the doctor said, «I'm off to get lunch, I'll see you at two o'clock and then we'll get the baby.» That is precisely what happened, and on the afternoon of 22 December we were holding in our arms our healthy baby boy, Leopold.

We liked the Engadine so much that we decided to stay. The paediatrician warned us: «The baby is allowed outside until minus 26 degrees. If the temperature drops any lower, he should stay inside.» Constantin and Leopold grew beautifully, protected by the mountain range. A short time later we found a house in Celerina that was still under construction, so we could still make some decisions on the final design according to our needs and wishes. This has been our second home since 1992.

When our children reached school age, they went to boarding school in Zuoz, and we would spend every weekend together in Celerina, which is only a few hours' drive from Milan. Here, there were so many family activities to enjoy and, depending on whether it was summer or winter, we would go skiing, cross-country skiing, cycling, swimming, hiking… This was the perfect place for us, although I have to admit that the Italian Dolomites are even more beautiful.

O SOLE MIO / KLAGENFURT, 1990

My twice-married friend Walter from Klagenfurt was telling me passionately about his new flame until he confessed: «She will only marry me on the condition that I carry her over the threshold of our new home after the ceremony.» The wedding was to take place within six months, he added with a look of despair. I could see only one way to save their union: a prefabricated house that could be built in two months. This is how I found myself designing my first timber house. Walter has since married his fourth wife.

It turned out not to be the only union arising from this story. A fruitful, constructive relationship grew between myself and the manufacturer, Adi Griffner, the owner of Griffner Holzhäuser. Together, we developed the house into a modular system and named it O Sole Mio, in reference to the sunlight. The large, fully glazed south-facing façade allows for significant amounts of light, while the wooden louvres facilitate heat control, enabling the house to be nearly energy self-sufficient when correctly oriented. This off-the-shelf design house became a bestseller in Europe.

I enthusiastically took on the job because I saw it as my chance to turn from a designer to an architect. However, as this was a prefab house project, I have had to curb my obsession with detail and refrain from designing the furniture. Apart from the bathroom and the kitchen, the choice of interiors was entirely up to the owners, who would bring in their own personality.

O Sole Mio catered for all budgets, but its affordability has now been compromised by the inflated cost of land. Perhaps not a bad thing. Somehow the overdevelopment of land must come to an end.

Sketch of the prefabricated house →
O Sole Mio, prefabricated home system →

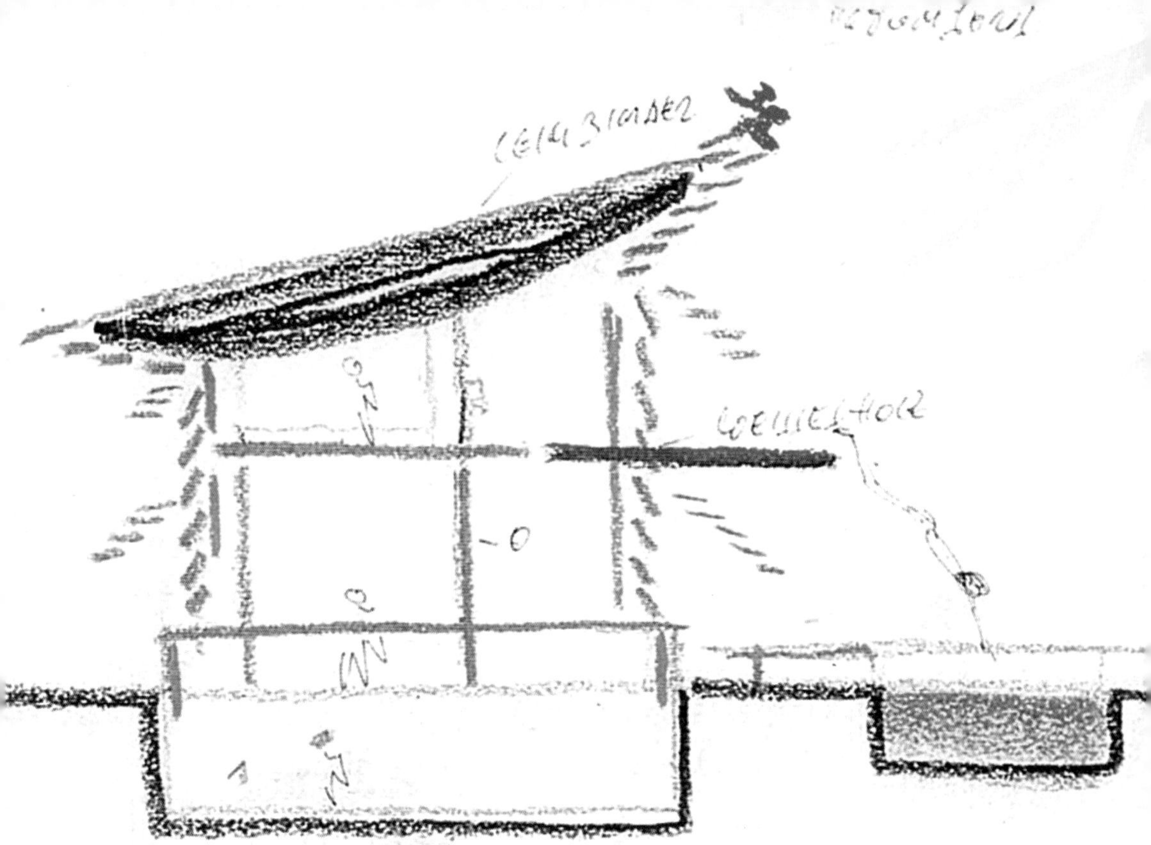
LEIMBINDER

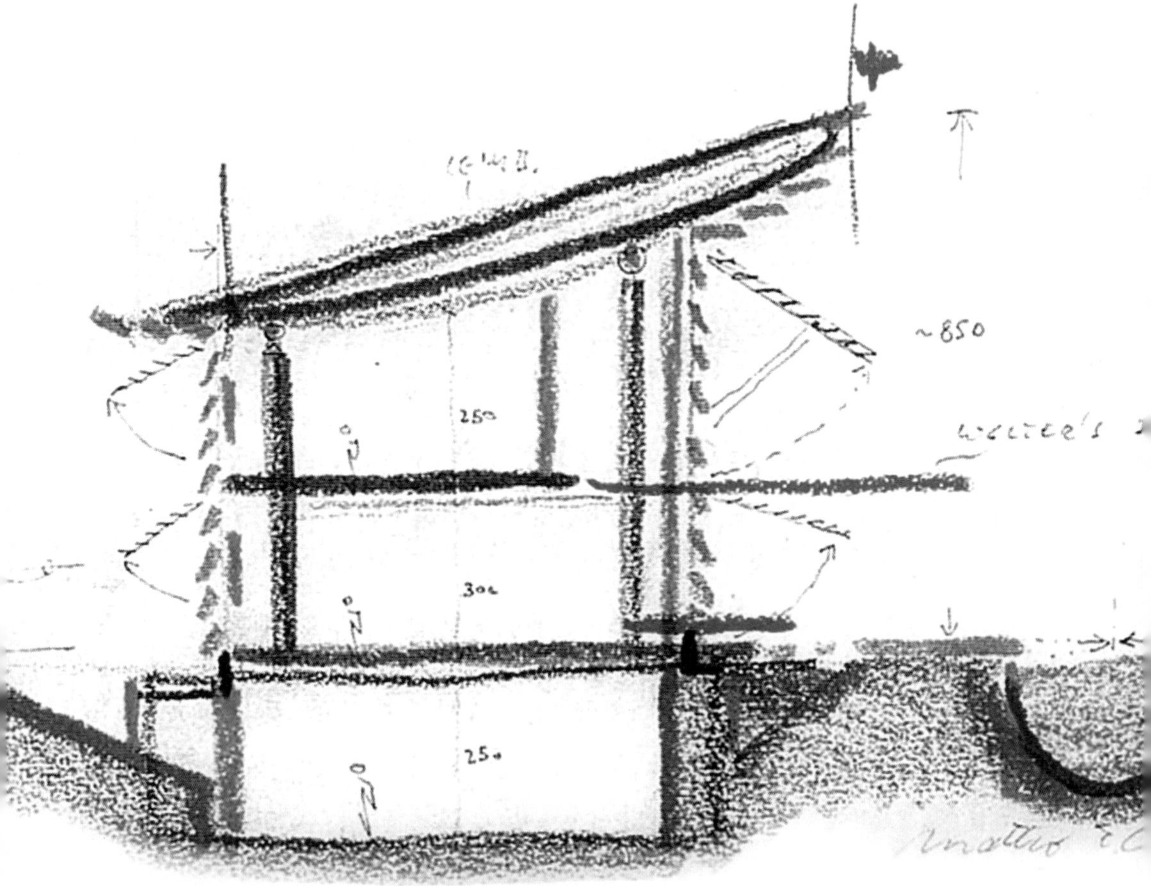
LEIM B.
~850
250
300
250

Skeleton racing involves riding down a frozen track, face down and head first, on a toboggan, and from the moment we arrived in the Engadine I was determined to get involved. The 1,212 metre natural ice track winds its way down from St. Moritz to Celerina, with a 157 metre drop in altitude. The St. Moritz Tobogganing Club (SMTC) is responsible for the upkeep of the track and is the guardian of the tradition of the Cresta Run, and of a very exclusive membership list.

My initial enthusiasm was soon tempered by the hurdles I had to overcome to become a member. Beginners' patience is tested with training sessions and endless pauses, spent staring at results on screens, like some sort of initiation ceremony. Once you complete the beginners' course, you become a Supplementary List Rider, or «SL,» and are finally allowed to stand by the track in the early hours of the morning, in the dark, wearing borrowed protective gear, in freezing winter temperatures, waiting to be called.

For years I set off from home in the early hours to go to St. Moritz, but I gradually developed ill-feelings towards the club and was about to give up the idea altogether until the wind changed and the legendary club secretary, Digby, suggested: **«Why don't you become a member?»**

I finally became a member in 1995 which allowed me to ride the track whenever I wanted and enjoy the experience to the full. Skeleton is a discipline you learn by doing and in your first runs you break from start to finish, just going a little faster each time. There are two starting points on the track, at the top or at the junction further down. If you start at the top, you ride at over a hundred kilometres per hour, constantly negotiating corners from which you can easily be ejected. I was never scared, but I was always respectful of the risk I was taking.

One Saturday morning, Susanne's gynaecologist called her from Samedan to reassure her: «Don't worry, your husband is safe with me.» This is not the sort of thing a woman expects to hear from her gynaecologist, but thankfully, he had been there for me when I flew off the skeleton track and crashed. He looked after me as I lay unconscious on the ice. I suffered a serious head injury, but that did not dampen my enthusiasm, which was so great that I later involved my two sons. Every year, on New Year's Eve or New Year's Day, there is a father-son Cresta race, and Constantin, Leopold and I raced several times. We even won once and received a trophy and the honour of having our names inscribed on the wall of the clubhouse, becoming part of its history.

Our excitement was proportional to Susanne's anxiety at the thought of the three of us going together. We became regulars at the orthopaedic clinic, to the extent that when Susanne rang to announce a new injury, she was simply asked which of the Thun men they would have the pleasure of seeing this time.

← Matteo on the skeleton track in the Engadine

PHILIPS KERAMAG / POTSDAM, 1991

The IFA, the world's largest trade fair for consumer electronics and home appliances, is held every year in Berlin and showcases the latest innovations in the industry. In 1991 all the exhibitors were German companies and Philips invited me to share my thoughts on the bathroom of the future. This gave me visions of a bathroom where the fittings and furniture were free to move, like animated characters in the form of toilets, showers, washbasins that interacted with people and even showed the daily news on the mirror, which isn't so unusual nowadays.

To produce the prototypes, I turned to the Babelsberg film studios in Potsdam, in the former East Germany, because their large workshops were known for producing large-scale stucco sculptures, notably a gigantic bust of Karl Marx. Perhaps these craftsmen, working in fiction, could also build an imaginary, visionary bathroom, so I went to meet them with my drawings. I had slept very badly in a smelly Berlin hotel when I arrived at the studios, but I was pleased to find that the classically trained sculptors and plasterers in Potsdam were interested in my ideological experiment to create a «new future.»

After the hard work came the pleasure. I got on well with the chief modeller and, as was usual in East Germany, he still had two jobs, one official at the film studios and one at Sanssouci Palace, where he was the head gardener. He offered to drive me around the palace grounds in his Trabi, and when he saw my delight at standing next to the papier-mâché Trabant painted pink and light blue, he suggested that I get behind the wheel, which I did. I drove confidently until he gripped the seat with both hands and shouted, «Slow down! Brake!» I was not sure why he was so nervous, as there was a level crossing ahead, but it was some distance away. «You have to pump the brakes!» I understood and began to pump them frantically until they actually started to slow us down. We stopped inches from the barrier. The journey was worth it, Sansouci Palace and its park are magnificent, I would even go as far as to say magical.

Bathrooms may sound unimportant to many, but they are unexpectedly challenging in projects. Take the SIDE Hotel, a decade later. The suites were to be fitted with large, freestanding baths, which posed considerable problems. These weigh one hundred kilograms dry and another two hundred and fifty when filled up with water. The structures had to be able to withstand this. Reducing the weight of bathrooms is therefore an architectural necessity.

The Murcia region in southeast Spain is full of almond plantations. There, powdered almond shells are used to make lightweight coffins. This material was transformative for the design of the hotel, and after all, the Japanese already use wooden bathtubs. I am a great admirer of ofuro, the narrow and tall wooden bathtubs in which they immerse themselves up to the lower lip, in the fetal position.

A preparatory sketch by Matteo Thun →
IFA Installation, Berlin, The Bathroom of the Future →

APHRODITE
HERRMANN
SIGFRIED

VILLA SCHNITZLER / VIENNA, 1991

Who wouldn't fall in love with a city where clocks tick to the beat of a waltz, business happens in coffee houses and sorrows are drowned in Sachertorte?

I was teaching at the University of Applied Arts in Vienna so we decided to move the whole family from Milan. We had the opportunity to rent the ground floor of Villa Schnitzler in Sternwartestrasse, the magnificent late 19th century house where Arthur Schnitzler wrote his masterpieces. Susanne organised the move and had a lorry loaded with all our things, Memphis pieces, Vorwerk carpets, lamps, sofas, crockery, vases, chairs, dressers, toys... everything we owned.

Our furniture looked wonderful in this new environment. We added colour wherever possible; Susanne even laid a vibrant Roy Lichtenstein carpet on the stairs leading to the inaccessible upper floors, and I painted dinosaurs in the children's bedrooms and redecorated the other rooms in green, blue, even red. But as beautiful as the villa was, and despite our best efforts to introduce finesse and colour, the living room remained irredeemably gloomy, covered as it was in dark wood panelling. Karel Schwarzenberg found the right words to describe the oppressive atmosphere that reigned in the room. Sitting down, he looked around and observed: **«This is not an apartment, this is a sarcophagus.»**

The boys, on the other hand, loved the large rooms where they could play freely with their tractors and trailers. Every Sunday, I took them to the nearby Observatory Park. However, as I watched them play on the swings, I found it depressing that there wasn't a friendly soul around to exchange a few words with. Susanne felt the same: «In Milan, the newsagent around the corner knows all about me within a couple of weeks. Here, it takes months just to be greeted.» We felt oppressed by the prevailing conservative mindset and shared the same longing for the openness, warmth and spontaneity we experienced in our life back in Milan. It simply was our emotional home.

After a year we still felt lost, so we decided to move back. Susanne organised a sale to avoid another monster move. She arranged all our objects and furniture into «lifestyle corners,» each with a different theme: City, Countryside, etc. For days, the society ladies flocked to our apartment for a viewing and soon all our possessions were marked with a red dot. Everything was sold, except for one vase. I was relieved when I came home to find that a ceramic piece by Ettore Sottsass with a price tag of one hundred shillings had been left behind. It is now worth around twenty thousand euros...

← Constantin and Leopold Thun

ARCHIMEDE SEGUSO / MURANO, 1992

I took my son Constantin to the workshop of Archimede Seguso in Murano. I had met him through Tiffany & Co. and decided to pay him a visit. Constantin was only three years old, but you are never too young to be fascinated by glass creatures made of fire and air. Seguso approached Tintin and asked: «Which animal would you like?» The boy replied, «un cavallino.» «Bene, allora facciamo un cavallino!» and the master glassblower began to create a little horse.

It soon became apparent why Seguso was considered the most talented glassblower on the island. A master glassblower works in the «*piazza*,» the area of the furnace where the production takes place, surrounded by three or four assistants who heat and reheat the glowing glass he is working on with tongs and various other tools to ensure that its temperature remains stable. For some pieces, however, the glass must be heated only once, hence the expression «*fatto alla prima*»—done at once. This requires speed, agility and a level of skill that can only be acquired through years of experience. In a single step, Seguso took the lump of glass from the oven and in a few seconds transformed it into a galloping horse. In Tintin's eyes, it was nothing short of a miracle.

Archimede Seguso's services to the city of Venice did not end with his craftsmanship. He was the first to raise the alarm when a fire broke out in the Teatro La Fenice on 29 January 1996. Living in Campo San Fantin, he had seen the first signs of the blaze from his bedroom window and alerted the fire brigade. «Come at once or my house will burn too!» Without his timely intervention, the fire would probably have spread to the entire neighbourhood, engulfing Venice's dense historic centre. But the firemen arrived in time, and the rest is history.

Archimede Seguso

VIGILIUS / LANA, 1999

The Vigiljoch overlooks Meran and attracts locals and tourists from all over the world. The hotel hosted eminent personalities, Willy Brandt and the Italian aristocracy have spent their holidays in this realm of woods and meadows. But the hotel's golden days were long gone when I toured the building with Ulrich Ladurner, who had just acquired it and was determined to save it from disrepair. I had asked my mother to accompany me and, in her golden Moon Boots, she followed me up the icy mountain path to the top station of the Jocher cable car, at an altitude of 1500 metres, where we were rewarded with a breathtaking view.

The visit lasted several hours and it became clear that the building was beyond repair. The majestic surroundings prompted me to suggest building something new, a building that would blend so discreetly into the landscape that it could hardly be noticed. The Vigilius Mountain Resort was born from this vision and has since become a model of contemporary alpine hospitality. Finally, nature was acknowledged as the dominant element; man's attempts to eclipse it usually fail. The building's reverence for nature extends beyond its appearance. It is energy self-sufficient, with local mountain farmers providing the wood chips that fuel the five-star hotel's energy needs. It stands as an example of conscious architecture, with zero-kilometre, zero CO^2, and zero waste construction and operation.

I am pleased to have prioritised the idyllic panorama over the architecture. Upon waking, still lying in bed, your vision spans from the Dolomites of South Tyrol on one side to the dense pine forest on the other, and you can feel a true sense of harmony with nature.

Inner balance is also paramount, so on arrival, guests are accommodated according to their individual needs. For example, those with low blood pressure, who tend to sleep longer in the morning, are given a room in the west wing, whilst early risers with high blood pressure tend to sleep better in the east wing. **My hope is that guests at the resort learn to appreciate the silence and the nature in a new way. Everything unimportant stays down in the valley. Life can be so simple.**

The new Vigilius designed by Matteo Thun →

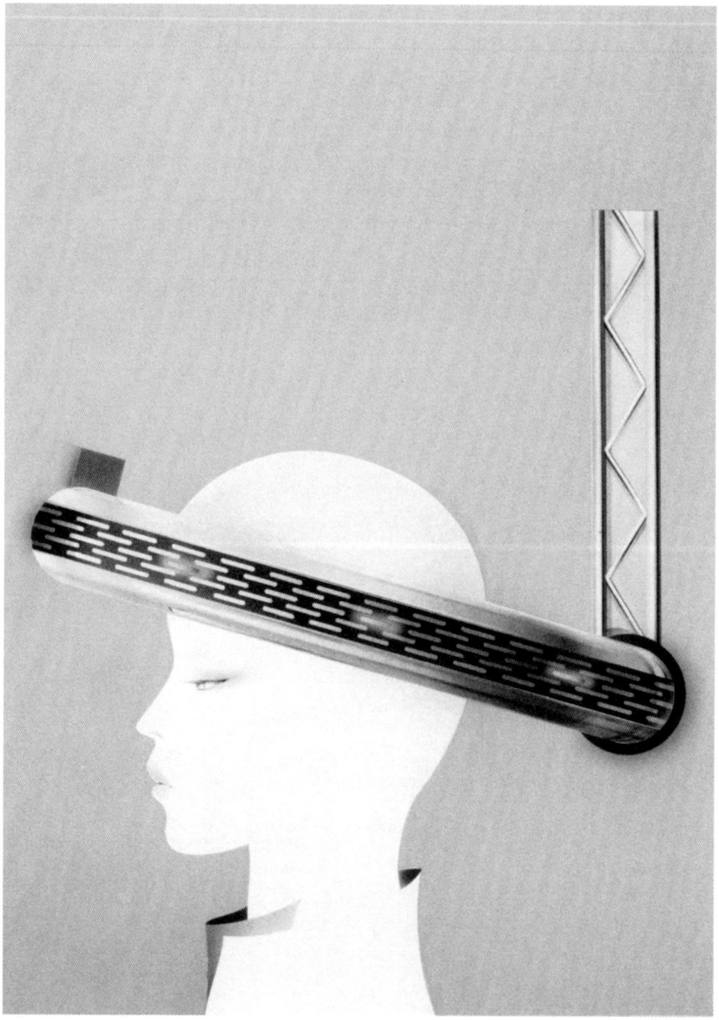

Hoodless hairdryer

TAKARA BELMONT / NEW YORK, OSAKA, 1995

I had never quite realised how many ways there are to dry and make your hair shine, until 1980 when working at Sottsass Associati on a new range of hairdryers and hoods for Wella. I spent significant time studying these appliances and eventually built-up considerable know-how in the field through my regular visits to the company's headquarters in Darmstadt, Germany, which supplies hair salons worldwide.

Years later, I was caught in a sudden downpour while strolling down 56th Street in New York. I had no umbrella so I found some shelter under a shop canopy. The rain showed no sign of stopping, so I entered the shop and asked if I could wait there until the storm had passed. The Japanese shop assistant understood little English and was clearly confused as to what I wanted: she sold hairdryers, but I did not seem to be interested in them—despite my soaking wet hair. At a loss, she called for her boss: «Boss is coming, boss is coming.» An elegant man appeared a few minutes later, and asked how he could help. **It turned out that I had unwittingly found refuge in the showroom of Takara Belmont, a world leader in hairdressing equipment from Osaka, and I was standing in front of the owner.** Our conversation led me to mention that I had designed a hairdryer hood for Wella. «Perhaps you could design one for us too,» he proposed. «Absolutely, I'd be delighted,» I responded, and we agreed to collaborate.

Back in Milan, I tinkered with various ideas. Among other things, I felt that women should not sit under a fixed hood that restricted their movement, so I worked on a system of free-standing radiating spotlights that could be positioned anywhere in the salon. A trip to Osaka to present the concept followed. As is customary in Japan, feedback was consistently positive, but in reality, the decision-making process was very slow. Japanese companies take decisions democratically, meaning that nothing can happen until a majority comes to a shared conclusion.

A year later, official approval for the Spotlight hairdryer stand arrived. I was compensated for the idea only to discover, two years on, starkly different models in use at hair salons. Japanese manufacturers seem to freely adapt and evolve someone's designs as they see fit.

PENSIONE AMERICA / FORTE DEI MARMI, 1992–1996

My parents used to take me to the Ritten near Bolzano for our summer holidays and Susanne and I were keen that our children built up memories of their own summer holiday location. Many Milanese used to go to Forte dei Marmi, a resort town with endless sandy beaches between Viareggio and La Spezia. An Italian Riviera children's paradise and the backdrop for endless memorable holiday snapshots, not least of parents dancing at the Capannina, the discotheque where all the popular singers used to perform on their summer tours.

We stayed at the Pensione America, right on the beach, and spent our days at their beach concession, Bagno America, with its rows of colourful parasols. The beach restaurant was run by Marcella, and we had the same pasta for lunch every day, followed by a *Dei Dei,* a delicious ice cream covered in chocolate that melted in our mouths as we basked in the sun.

Highlights of our days at the seaside included playing marbles on the beach, digging tracks in the soft white sand by pulling the children by their arms and legs and leaving their bottoms to do the rest. Leopold's bottom was particularly suited to this exercise. The eldest, Constantin, usually led the game, followed closely by little Leopold, until I struck the final blow. On a calm day with no waves, we hired a *moscone* to row along the coast. One of the two hulls filled with water and the ship began to lean to one side. With two boys on board who could not swim, we had to be rescued by the lifeguard.

The guests of the Pensione America all gathered at seven o'clock in the large restaurant for dinner. The two elderly sisters who ran the pension also served the food, while keeping an ear out for the only telephone available, hidden under the stairs. When it rang, everyone would turn around, hoping the call was for them. The chosen one would proudly get up and walk across the room to answer. The food in Forte dei Marmi was tasty, although not as good as in the nearby Apennines. The children loved it, and relished the mornings when we'd take them on bikes to the bakery for fresh *focaccine.*

The pine forest and its miniature racetrack was the town's and our favourite place to spend the evening. Five minutes cost one hundred lira and the laps in mini electric Ferraris were electrifying. One year we took two of Constantin and Leopold's school friends with us on holiday, and on the way we made a pit stop at the Maranello circuit, where we bought them a Ferrari Formula Uno outfit. Back in the *pineta*, their lap times had improved considerably. As our holiday came to an end and we were heading back to Milan, I gave in to their request to speed on the motorway. We made it back in no time but the boys gave me away and, justifiably, I was told off by their mothers for putting their precious life in danger.

Bagno America

SIDE HOTEL / HAMBURG, 1999–2000

How does a love story begin? That's right, with a great story. This happened to me in 1999 when for the first time I was asked to design the interiors of a city hotel. The architect, Jan Störmer, had designed the building in two interlocking elements with two cantilevered suite floors. Through a constructive exchange of ideas and specifications drawn to the last detail, we developed a symbiotic architectural and interior design for one of Europe's first design hotels.

The central focal point was to be a thirty-metre-high atrium, which would serve as the heart and foyer of the hotel. To be honest, I wasn't quite sure I wanted this to be the defining feature of the hotel, but at the time Robert Wilson was staging a play at the Thalia Theatre, so I contacted the acclaimed director and set designer in the hope that he would help with the lighting scheme for the atrium. He suggested we meet at the bar of the Four Seasons Hotel at midnight. With the help of a substantial amount of vodka, we had the lighting concept ready by six in the morning. Unfortunately, the client had a different perspective and was not prepared to spend for any extras. «If you want him, you'll have to pay the theatre director yourself,» was his response. I footed the bill and the design, borne by our sleepless night, continues to attract visitors. I was very pleased with the result.

My ten-year-old son Leopold was less pleased on the day of the opening. He was sitting with Susanne on the custom-made Supersassi sofa in the upstairs foyer. **«I think this house is awful. Can I tell that to dad?»** he whispered into his mum's ear. He gave me his honest opinion later that evening. I took note of it, mindful that a boy is bound to see things from a fresh, new perspective. The next day, however, he took it back and told me: «I've changed my mind, the house isn't as bad as I said yesterday.» He had looked at it in more detail and had changed his mind. The following year, the SIDE was voted best hotel in Germany and awarded the Design Hotel seal for its innovative design.

How does a true love story end? That's right, it never does. My relationship with the hospitality industry now spans over two decades and has resulted in the completion of over eighty projects. I have poured my heart and soul into each and every one of them.

← The Side Hotel in Hamburg, architecture by Jan Störmer

UNCLE JOSI AND AUNT TESI / MILAN, 2000

My uncle Josi Thun was married to aunt Tesi Crespi, an elegant, extravagant and fun-loving woman, for whom this was her second marriage. When Josi died, she had him cremated in view of taking the ashes to his birthplace, Castel Fondo, which was also going to be his final resting place. She asked Susanne to drive her and the urn from Milan to Val di Non.

When they stopped at a motorway café, the precious parcel could not be left unattended in the car, so Aunt Tesi took it inside and placed it on the bar counter while she drank her espresso, fully dressed in black, including a large black hat. Then they set off again and, thanks to Susanne, what was left of Uncle Josi arrived safely at destination.

Tesi was over eighty years old, but she wasn't prone to sadness. She soon went through her telephone book to see who of her childhood friends might still be available. She found that Paolo Caccia Dominioni seemed to be alive and well. She rang him, made an appointment—and married him.

All went according to her plans. Susanne was to be maid of honour at the wedding, and she received an invitation to Palazzo Caccia Dominioni, the beautiful residence in Piazza Sant'Ambrogio designed in the 1950s by Paolo's brother, the architect Luigi Caccia Dominioni. Susanne was shown into the dressing room of the new lady of the house. There were elaborate, locked wardrobes filled with wonderful pieces of fashion. But the real treasures lay on the inside of the door panels, where Tesi had pasted numerous photographs of men with bare chests. Her collection of handsome men was her pride and joy, and Susanne can count herself among the very few who to have had the honour of viewing it.

Aunt Tesi's closet

SUMMER HOLIDAYS / RITTEN, 1992–2000

I have wonderful memories of my childhood summer holidays. For many years, my cousins, my brother and I would spend the summer on the Ritten, the mountains north of Bolzano. In Italy, the school holidays last more than three months, so with each school report came dozens of weeks of carefree time in Klobenstein. **We built tall tree houses from which the world seemed so much smaller, we explored the woods or brewed chestnut beer, which looked as awful as it tasted and that's why no one wanted to drink it.**

The Sunday 10 o'clock mass was not to be missed. Our favourite uncle, Sepp, would take us up to the choir, from where we would break out in concerts of fart noises, which earned us disapproving looks from below.

Susanne and I wanted our children to share our cheerful experience of summer holidays in the mountains, so in 1992 we rented a holiday house in the village of Maria Himmelfahrt on the Ritten, a tiny settlement with no more than a dozen summer houses.

The time we spent together in nature was wonderful for me, and I hope the children have the same memories. We built cable cars that went up and down the cedar trees, we carved rods to go fishing in the toad pond next to the house, and Leopold and Constantin rehearsed entire theatre plays to perform for the Toggenburg goats.

We enjoyed a month of nothing but family.

WMF / GEISSLINGEN, 1984–2000

When I left Sottsass Associati in Ferragosto 1983 to start my own business, my order book was empty, but my mind was full of ideas and I was confident that quality would prevail and everything would turn out well. A year later I was relieved when WMF knocked on my door. The head of Württembergische Metallwarenfabrik hoped to bring the innovative Memphis drive to the German industry and develop a new design language common to all household metalware, from tableware to kitchen utensils. I was excited at the prospect of being involved and designing new cutlery, kitchen utensils, pots and kitchen knives. WMF was a leader in the household goods sector, with more than 100 company-owned stores in Germany alone.

When I travelled to Stuttgart for meetings, Mr. Meichle, a bulky driver, used to pick me up at the airport late in the evening and drive me at full speed down the autobahn to Geisslingen an der Steige. I once asked him if he wasn't afraid of speed traps: «Not at all. I am known to the police.» Besides his taxi business, he ran a funeral company.

We have tried hard with WMF to bring innovation to people, but have come to the conclusion that it does not work. At least not to the extent we would have liked. We did manage to do some things without making too many concessions to the mainstream market, one of which is the bestselling 30-piece Balance cutlery set. Cutlery items are very intimate objects that became a hobby of mine. I could spend days designing knife blades. In my spare time I even designed a pop cutlery set to send to Madonna for her birthday.

After sixteen sweet years of collaboration, our business relationship came to a bitter end at the beginning of 2000. We went to present some new kitchen appliances and the four company engineers there concluded, «We'll think about your proposals with a view to sending them into production in two to three years' time.» Boom. The industry never waits that long to make a decision, a product manager is either convinced or drops the idea. I never saw WMF again.

← The WMF cutlery designed for Madonna

VAPIANO / HAMBURG, 2000

It's no secret that I love Italian food. While we were working on the construction site of the SIDE Hotel, we all got hungry for pasta and went to what was supposed to be the best «Italian» in Hamburg. I ordered a simple *spaghetti al pomodoro* but was served a tomato soup with spaghetti swimming in it. With the best will in the world, I couldn't bring myself to eat it, so I sent the plate back untouched, not expecting the manager to come back to enquire why. I looked up and smiled, «I'm sorry, I'm from South Tyrol, I live in Italy... I am used to my mother's spaghetti.»

The exchange sparked a conversation around the table, and one of the colleagues was adamant that there had to be a way to turn spaghetti into a real business. He then mentioned an interesting development in the market, Pasta Espresso, which used an innovative way of preparing pasta that only took a few minutes. The foundations were laid for the first Vapiano on Hohe Bleichen in Hamburg, and together we founded the new Italian restaurant chain. I was also responsible for the interior design and styling concept.

The idea was simple and initially successful. Vapiano served pasta, risotto, pizza and salads prepared on the spot. **It was fast food with a commitment to slow food quality.** The name Vapiano is a contraction of «va piano,» Italian for «slow down.»

I had the best of intentions when one evening in Berlin, where we were celebrating the opening of the Intercity Hotel for which we had designed the interiors, it was getting late and I invited the daughter of the owner of the hotel chain for a pizza at Vapiano, just opposite the train station. Much to my embarrassment, I had to admit that the pizza was... *so-so*.

The first Vapiano in Hamburg →

VAPIANO
CARBONARA
Oberssauce,
Ei, Speck
SALSICCIA
CON FICHI
Scharfe italienische Wurst,
Feigen, Tomatensauce
SALAMI E RUCOLA
CON RICOTTA
Rucola, Pinienkerne, Salami,
Ricotta, Weisswein
TACCHINO PICCANTE
Hühnerbrust, Orangen-Chili-Sauce,
Pak-Choi, Paprika
FUNGHI
Pilze,
Oberssauce
PESTO
Basilikum-Pesto, Olivenöl,
Pinienkerne
PESTO CON SPINACI
PANCETTA BRIE
CRUDO E FICHI
PASTASORTEN
VOLLKORNPASTA
PESTO
SALAMI E RUCOLA
CON RICOTTA
SCAMPI
PASTASORTEN

ROSETTA / CAPRI, 2000–2022

Our good friends invited us to Capri for a birthday party. The Neapolitan writer Raffaele La Capria had built an enchanting house on the side of Monte Solaro, the tallest mountain on the island. The house was completely integrated into the hillside. From below you could only see two white columns, from the sea you couldn't see it at all. We spent a wonderful day and when Rosetta, who had cooked us dinner, left at 10 o'clock, I asked her out of the blue: «Rosetta, is the house downstairs still for sale?» It was a long, very long shot, I had no idea if there was actually a property down there. «Oh, you mean the one that belonged to the farmer's wife who died a week ago?» inquired Rosetta. «Yes, that's exactly what I mean.»

Cupid had shot an arrow and it hit me in the heart the next morning. After breakfast I went back to Monte Solaro to explore and jumped over the fence of the property below. I had a good look around and called Susanne, who agreed: **«Let's buy it right away!»** It was a Sunday, so we had to save our excitement for the next day. On Tuesday we completed the purchase of a house that we would enjoy for the next 23 years.

But there were many hurdles to overcome before we could move in. The farmer's wife had been living in a very small space with a donkey and a few chickens. We had to adapt and extend the property, walking a legal tightrope. In Capri you are not allowed to enlarge a window or even knock down a wall, let alone add rooms. The pool was even more difficult. To get permission to build it, I went to the heritage office in Naples. The socialist superintendent at the time despised Capri's exclusivity and it took years to get permission to build it, but we did it. Surrounded by orange, lemon and olive trees, we had created a little piece of heaven—which we sold in 2023.

How could we? From spring and throughout the summer, Capri is bursting at the seams. The number of visitors arriving daily from the mainland in search of a postcard view is out of all proportion to the island's capacity. Overtourism has made it impossible to go round the island and at Easter you can't move an inch in the Piazzetta. The waiter at our favourite café had been welcoming us nicely for twenty years, but now it was just a «What would you like to drink?». Our favourite restaurant was now charging us €285 for two salads and two glasses of prosecco. We began to wonder if we were in the right place. We had a family meeting and with a heavy heart we decided to leave Capri.

← The Thun gem property on Capri

JULIUS MEINL / VIENNA, 1985

Julius Meinl's excellent coffees and fine teas are favoured by Austria's connoisseurs. I once visited Julius Meinl IV in his office in Vienna. **A fire burned all year round in the open fireplace that dominated the imposing room, no matter how hot the weather might be.** I went to see him to ask whether he would accept to host an exhibition of coffee pots and cups produced by my students at the Academy of Applied Arts at the *K. and K. Hofzuckerbäckerei Demel.* It seemed to me that this historic coffee house on the Graben, an unmissable stop for visitors in Vienna, was the ideal place for this. He agreed.

His son, Julius V, has been a friend of our family for a long time. I once suggested to him that the Moor, the company's trademark, looked too submissive and sad and that he should be younger and happier. As a result, we worked together on a new logo, new coffee cups, and in general on Meinl's entire corporate identity.

Every child in Austria now knows not only the Meinl Moor, but also the mouthwatering Meinl Mozartkugeln. Following his acquisition of the largest producer of these iconic chocolate balls, we helped Julius V to launch his modern reinterpretation of this classic with a new name, Mozart Koogles, a new spicy graphic design and new flavours—nougat, coffee, orange, lychee, and a champagne edition for Christmas. A delicious task all-round.

Coffee cup designed for Julius Meinl →

SIX MEMOS

FOR THE NEXT MILLENNIUM

1 - Lightness
2 - Quickness
3 - Exactitude
4 - Visibility
5 - Multiplicity
6 - Consistency

SIX MEMOS FOR THE NEXT MILLENNIUM / MILAN, 2000

Every Italian knows Italo Calvino. His works are taught in schools and are deeply rooted in the national consciousness.

His «*Six Memos for the Next Millennium*» was a revelation for me. The book is a collection of lectures he was to give at Harvard, in which he describes the qualities of the great literature of the past in order to define universal values for the future: lightness, speed, precision, visibility, multiplicity and, finally, consistency. The sixth memo exists only in title, Calvino died before writing it and he never saw the new millennium.

The values applied to literature, but they reverberated with my creative approach in other fields: «**My activity has mostly consisted of reducing weight; now I have tried to reduce the weight of human figures, now of celestial bodies, now of cities;** above all, I have tried to reduce the weight of the structure of the narrative and of language.»

This attempt at simplification perfectly describes the process I go through when designing a building or an object. And also the inevitable clash that arises between desire and reality: «I soon realised that there was a gulf between the facts of life, which should have been my raw materials, and the quick, light touch I wanted for my writing,» Calvino adds.

He saw quality in the speed of the flashes of inspiration that come to the gifted, in the instantaneous capture of an artistic intuition, as well as in the «*agility, mobility, informality*» of a prompt style. Every creative individual longs for this inhibition and mental agility that makes everything possible.

I will never forget the moment when I saw my world in the form of a book. We have now entered the next millennium and these qualities have become a natural trait of our contemporary consciousness.

← Italo Calvino's memos

LEOPOLD'S LYCEUM / ZUOZ, 2002

Back in 1998 on the day Constantin left Milan to Zuoz to attend the Lyceum Alpinum, Leopold swore allegiance to his mother: «I will remain faithful to you and stay with you in Milan at the German School.»

On Leopold's last day at school before the summer holidays, the excited children were playing football in the playground when the ball landed on a tree. Leopold climbed up to grab it and it all went very quickly from the moment he fell and hit the ground very badly.

Susanne was immediately alerted and she took him to the nearest hospital. It was a very hot day and the hospital building was no cooler. Leopold had several fractures in his forearms and in his hands and was in terrible pain, of which the doctor was well aware. Nevertheless, he said he had no way of operating on him there and then advised, as I arrived at the hospital, that it would be better to take him elsewhere. This seemed like another task for the Gut Klinik in St. Moritz so I asked for painkillers and placed Leopold in the Porsche. We were there in a record time of two hours. As usual, Susanne had announced us and we were seen immediately. Half an hour later Leopold was on the operating table.

The operation went well, but Leopold had both arms in plaster and could not even hug me back as I cuddled him upon his waking from the anesthetics. For the whole summer the boy could neither eat or get dressed without help. We revised our holiday plans so that he could have a reasonably good holiday despite the circumstances and decided to go to Capri. His grandmother came along and we all stayed at the Hotel Luna, where everyone was very attentive to our little patient and bowing to his every wish, even to be driven around by his grandma in a little electric car.

Towards the end of the holiday the casts were removed back at the Engadine clinic and Susanne enrolled him on the summer English course in Zuoz. Leopold liked the environment so much that he decided to try out the Lyceum. Coming back on his promise to his mum, he had hardly left the Director's office when he rang her to confess: **«I'm sorry mum, I'm staying in Zuoz.»** We now had two boys attending the Lyceum Alpinum, far away from their home in Milan.

Chesa Comunela in Zuoz

CHICCO

CARS / 1970–2004

I got my first car in 1970, a mustard yellow Fiat 128 bought from my aunt for 400,000 lire. That's not quite true, because my father paid for it on the promise that I would never ride a motorbike. I kept motocross bikes out of the deal, but that is another story.

The first Fiat 128 was soon replaced by a Fiat 128 Rally, with alloy wheels, a Ceccato carburetor, and a sports exhaust, which increased my desire for speed and the sheer joy of driving.

I look back on my love of cars in a positive light. When my brother was fifteen, he dreamed of becoming a racing driver, so we decided to try our luck together and volunteered as assistants at the Jim Russell Racing School at the Salzburgring. The following year we took matters into our own hands and raced our Formula Ford cars in Zeltweg.

We scrimped and saved all we could for our hobby. We slept in a tent, and ate noodles for lunch and dinner for days on end, cooked on a camping stove. It wasn't great, but it was worth it: we were living the dream. With our savings we bought tyres and petrol, and I even managed to buy a Simca Rally, which I spruced up to take part in rally hillclimbs, not entirely successfully.

Then my mother gave me a Citroen DS. She believed that the bodywork of this French «goddess» would protect me in the event of an accident. The seats were modelled on sofas and were so comfortable that on occasions I fell asleep on the motorway. It is a blessing that nothing bad ever happened.

In 1998 I switched to a Mercedes 190 diesel, shifting later to a Porsche Carrera 4, much to the delight of my two sons. Then, to their disappointment, I sold it six years later. Although it was perfectly designed and a speedaholic's dream, I could no longer reconcile driving it with my approach to architecture and design. **Consciousness is not only a professional message; it has to be lived holistically.**

Since then, I move around Milan either on foot or on a folding bike. I've chosen it carefully for its gear ratio and chain cover, so that my trousers don't get dirty before meetings: I admit I do hop on and off pavements to cheat Milan's one-way streets. Many of the office staff also cycle to work. When I am up in the Engadine, I use my mountain bike and ride countless kilometers—emitting zero CO_2.

← Matteo mit Constantin in Fuorcla Surlej

HUGO BOSS / COLDRERIO, 2006

Where should a listed fashion company go to free its creative minds? Maybe Paris, Milan, or London? No, Hugo Boss chose Coldrerio, a Swiss village near the Italian border. Our brief was to design the brand's new headquarters, where the stylists would feel at home developing collections that would be produced and sold worldwide.

There were two managing directors at their head office, one looking after finance, the other was in charge of creative. The latter wanted to know what kind of style I had in mind for their new headquarters, and I ventured, too lightly, «The opposite of an Audi TT.» An awkward silence followed before he stated: «I was the one responsible at Audi to develop the TT.» Oh dear, I couldn't find a single suitable excuse for my remark but, thankfully, eventually all turned out well.

We had a glass building in mind, wrapped in a shading wooden lattice that would not only represent the weaving of textiles, but also bring the building into harmony with the landscape. We developed the project working with an Austrian timber construction company, and completed in a very short time a three-storey building with generous open spaces. The open-plan offices were fully flexible, organised only using partitions, and a sheltered balcony wrapped the floors around the contours of the building. I thought it was important for creative people to be able to step outside, be it to smoke or for a breath of fresh air, while remaining close to their colleagues.

Despite the bumpy start with the Audi TT, we were all happy with the result, especially the employees, who felt a higher level of freedom in their creative process. It all went so well that we went on to design their flagship store in New York. It is located in the Meatpacking District in a former butcher's shop, which led me to introduce the same wooden lattice on the bare industrial walls on which to hang the clothes: passion for fashion replaced love for meat. That said, my Milanese fashion upbringing meant I could not accept any of the suits I was kindly offered.

Hugo Boss headquarters in Switzerland →

«The soul of the place» is the common thread running through all our architectural projects. We always aim to respect the genius loci and we let it guide us in our design process.

I was offered the opportunity to design a holiday village on the Katschberg pass in Austria. When I arrived in Carinthia for the site visit, cows were grazing on the green meadow where approximately sixty chalets were planned to be built. I was informed that in winter the children of the area skied there. «Where will the cows go in the summer and the children in winter when the meadow is gone?» It appeared that no one had thought that far ahead.

I began thinking about the location and suggested there were more desirable outcomes. How about building two towers on the edge of the meadow? I was told that the Fire Authority would never approve any high-rise on the Katschberg because it would not comply with their strict guidelines for evacuation routes. I was strongly advised to drop the idea but, instead, I involved the Governor of Carinthia: «Mr. Haider, would you please contact the mayor of Katschberg and ask him to speak to the head of the Fire Authority? I want to build two towers.»

The two monoliths jutting out of the mountainous landscape have become landmarks of the region. They are clad in larch wood and connected to a biomass energy power plant. The residents of the towers have a 360-degree view of the Katsch Valley and of Salzburg's Lungau. Unfortunately, the cows no longer graze on the meadow and the children no longer ski there; another holiday village was built on the ski slope.

Building in the Alps is complex. I am not calling for a halt to construction, but for a new attitude that encourages renovation and restoration. Of course, old structures must be adapted to the expectations of modern travellers, but we must not become slaves to tourism. That is why I believe it is preferable to limit the number of visitors allowed in some areas, for example the Dolomite passes. The beauty of the Alps does not lie in its buildings, but in the landscape, where people should enjoy the feeling of freedom given by wide open spaces.

← Kitsch and Katsch, Katschberg

ZWILLING / SOLINGEN, SHANGHAI, 2006–2024

My first meeting with the Shanghai subsidiary of German brand Zwilling, was with the managing director, Mr. Ma, who had a solid reputation for being a genius. He began by explaining the logic of Chinese department stores, which follow a completely different one to those in Germany or Italy. In China, it would not be unusual for female office workers go to a shopping centre during their lunch break to test, say, a cooking pot, which they would happily purchase after a demonstration. An interesting foretaste of how my collaboration with Zwilling would later develop.

Ma Lifeng had managed to make things work much faster than the parent company in Germany. He achieved this by hiring German engineers, who were thrilled to find out that the «Can't do, it doesn't work» they knew only too well back home, had become «Sure, let's try» in Shanghai. They were happy and motivated, and much more productive as a result.

My partner Antonio Rodriguez and I worked together developing products for Zwilling. The secret to the success of this venture has been twofold: first, we were not afraid of imitation, we just needed to innovate faster than those trying to copy and keep coming up with new products. Second, teamwork with Chinese partners and colleagues works flawlessly once you have gained their trust. But that can take years.

In China we have been most active in product design. For Zwilling, we develop high-end knives, pots and cookware, as well as small electrical appliances. To be as close to the market as possible, we rented an office on the top floor of a historic building owned by the governing Chinese Communist Party. The building has a roof terrace overlooking the Pudong district that we used for press events. Before we held our first event, the wife of the building's concierge, who had full control over the building, intervened. Our plan was too dangerous, someone could fall off the terrace, so it was essential that we hired official supervisors, which the concierge was only too happy to provide. From then on, ten supervisors oversaw all our product launches, for a not inconsiderable fee. They would stand in each corner of the roof terrace whilst most of our guests wondered what these gentlemen were there for. For us, they became a sort of good luck charm, essential for the success of the new products being launched.

We closed our Shanghai office at the start of the pandemic. Our staff working there moved to Milan and, like their colleagues in Munich, they are key to our ability to work internationally.

Zwilling knives, collection 1731 →

FIJI WATER / ANDORRA, 2008

One of the wealthiest women in Spain had chosen me to design a whole neighbourhood for her. Among other places, she had properties in Andorra, where I found myself in a beautiful narrow valley, closed within the Pyrenees' massive and barren mountains that seemed to be guarding and protecting the independent principality. The site in question was on the northern edge of the capital, Andorra la Vella. The project appealed to me on several levels: the political complexity of being a tax haven sandwiched between France and Spain, the geographical peculiarity of the location with its dramatic drops in altitude, and the social and practical implications of urban planning an entire neighbourhood.

Things got off to a good start, and to cement our business relationship I invited her to our Milan office. During our meeting she made no secret of where her top priorities lay: reduced energy consumption and, above all, draconian management of water resources. **Andorra and the surrounding mountains are almost completely devoid of vegetation, so water management is very important there.** Following hours discussing this important topic, we understood well and were enthused by her environmental approach. I invited her for lunch. Before we had even sat down at the restaurant next to our office, our friendly waiter poured some bottled Fiji water. My guest looked at him, then at me, and said: «I don't think you understand what this is all about.» It didn't matter that I had no influence on the doings of our diligent waiter; she was beside herself and decided to leave.

Although we never heard from her again, I still have a glimmer of hope that I am the right man for her ambitious project. One morning while admiring an Egyptian oasis, I drew my vision for the new district in Andorra. Who knows, perhaps one day...

← Sketch of Residential Tower in Andorra

WALTER PFEIFFER / CAPRI, 2008

Off the coast of Positano, halfway to Capri, three small islands form the Li Galli archipelago. They once belonged to Russian dancer Rudolf Nureyev. Today we are fortunate to count the current art-loving owners amongst our friends.

Walter Pfeiffer announced he was visiting Capri. We had met him through our son Constantin, who had been a student of the celebrated Swiss photographer at the *école cantonale d'art de Lausanne*. He arrived with a digital camera, a technology he said did not convince him, so he had fun experimenting, photographing anything from espresso cups to kitchen knives and sink taps, until we finally managed to turn his attention to the breathtaking beauty of Capri.

For Walter, Nureyev was not only the most gifted dancer of the 20th century, he was his idol, so we decided to pay homage to him by visiting the Li Galli archipelago that had been so dear to him. We set off on our boat, anchored it between the three islands and jumped into the sea to swim ashore to our friends' house on Gallo Lungo.

After a few strokes, Walter began yelling: «I'm dying! I'm dying!» I took his calling seriously and went to grab him to try and keep him afloat. I looked at him surprised at his grinning as he said, «I think that I am dead.» The distress was caused by a jelly fish sting. It hurts like hell, but the poisonous tentacles are, fortunately, nowhere near life-threatening.

We reached the island slowly and with great effort, as Walter willingly abandoned himself to the current, believing, or pretending, that he was actually dead. We dragged him over the rocks like a sack of potatoes, leaving a bruise on his shin. That was it, with the sight of blood he confirmed he was irretrievably dead.

Our visit to Nureyev's dream estate fell through as result. So many opportunities are not lived up to when one, only too easily, declares to be «dead.»

Walter Pfeiffer →

VENERE BIANCA / MONTELUPO FIORENTINO, 2009

As a boy I was fascinated by how a lump of clay, loam and water could be transformed into the most beautiful of shapes with the help of a wheel. My interest for ceramics had begun over half a century ago. It flared up again in 2009 when I set out to design full architectural concepts, comprising of all details, down to self-designed hand-thrown terracotta vases.

Going to Montelupo Fiorentino feels like a pilgrimage for ceramic lovers. For centuries, the aristocratic families of this town on the Arno River have had their houses filled with clay decorations. Ettore Sottsass also appreciated the masters of the potter's wheel, and one night, when he was admitted to a hospital in Palo Alto, California, driven by death hallucinations, he designed a ceramics collection he named *le ceramiche delle tenebre*, which he later had produced in Montelupo Fiorentino.

I wanted to feel the authentic Montelupo craftsmanship with my own hands, so I went to Tuscany to meet two seasoned local potters. At first, they turned me down: **«We don't take orders anymore, we're retiring.» «You can't, I need you!»** I pleaded. I took the two retiring men to dinner, and we became friends over a glass of wine. One of them began telling me how he had started his career, inspired by the beauty of a woman. When he was eighteen, he went to a strip club where a former Miss Tuscany was performing an elaborate dance on stage to the flickering lights of a sensual film. She became the object of desire that he knew he could never reach. Her stage name was *Venere Bianca*, White Venus. When he realised that marrying her would remain a pipe dream, he channelled all his passion into creating masterful ceramics. I named the collection that resulted from these late dinner confessions *Venere Bianca*, in homage to his unfulfilled romantic dream.

← Ceramic pieces by Matteo Thun

NIVEA / HAMBURG, 2012–2018

Tradition can be both a blessing and a curse. NIVEA had solid foundations to look to the future with confidence, with over a century of presence in hundreds of countries, and more than fifty products developed by 1290 scientists conducting 1700 studies a year, none of them using animal testing. In 2012 we became their lead design agency to develop their new communication and packaging strategy. This entailed first coming to terms with the brand's history, which was carefully enshrined in the company's own museum and archives. The goal was, after all, to return the brand to its golden days of the fifties and sixties.

NIVEA cream has left its mark on the collective memory of consumers. The tin is blue, the lettering is white, as is the content. As anyone who knows us can guess, we focused primarily on their trademark colour and set out to soften the original cold Prussian blue by replacing it with a gentler Parisian night blue—this was only the first step of many developments we had in mind for the brand.

Staying true to NIVEA's innovative spirit, we maintained a contemporary approach while ensuring that all sub-brands remained distinctly identifiable as belonging to the «mother brand.» I must acknowledge that while the ideas were ambitious, their implementation was only partially successful. Germany is known for its meticulous risk management, which extends to the smallest detail. In this instance, it resulted in an excessive delay between product development and launch. Economic realism tends to lead to delayed responses, whereas flexibility and speed are paramount. My biggest hurdle in working with German companies has often been the so-called «acceptance test,» where a product is tested and retested until the inevitable conclusion is reached that everything should stay as it is. For some branding experts, this may seem the easiest way, but design cannot work like this. **Successful entrepreneurial risk-taking requires a spirit of innovation coupled with courage—you can't have one without the other.**

Colour studies for Nivea →

SATURATED
WD
CS 041
WD
CD 01
WS 01
CD
3
CS 01
CS 03
NIVEA SHADES OF BLU
WS
WD

17

MOSELLE WINE / LONGUICH, 2012

I found an envelope on my desk with a handwritten letter from a young couple of winemakers from the Moselle. «When people have had wine at our winery, they shouldn't drive home, they should have somewhere to stay, but we have nowhere to put them up. We have little or no funds, but could you help us in any way?»

I thought it was a colleague's joke and binned the letter, only to have a pang of conscience later: What if the story was true? I should at least call them and find out. A short time later I had the couple on the phone. They explained that they wanted to build a small hotel and asked if I would come to Longuich on the Mosel. The place is in the middle of nowhere. When I eventually arrived in Rhineland-Palatinate I discovered a beautiful landscape. The Moselle valley is full of huge apple trees, seven to eight metres high. As far as the eye can see, the steep slopes are covered with the vines for which the area is famous. The couple grew them on wires, like climbers.

I could not bring myself to introduce a hotel in this charming valley. I made my position clear, «I am sorry, even if you were granted permission, it can't happen with me.» «Is there an alternative?» they asked. I had seen small stone huts up on the hill among the vines, where the winegrowers go to rest at lunchtime, to recover from their hard work and find shelter from the summer heat. **«We could build winegrowers' cottages, each with a guest room,»** I suggested instinctively.

They both thought it was a great idea but doubted that a bank would ever finance such an unusual plan: «It costs a lot more to build twenty cottages than a single building with twenty rooms, but we can always try.» It took a year to convince their bank of the potential. They were backing something unique, something that had never been done in the area.

The twenty-square-metre houses were built in local stone. They have a very simple layout and are sparsely furnished. Each cottage has its own garden, which guests are invited to care for during their stay. Fresh yoghurt is delivered for breakfast, which they complement with strawberries picked from «their» garden. The same goes for the flowers, which they can cut to decorate their cottage as they wish.

The project soon found resonance and went on to win the German Prize for Architecture and the German Prize of Rural Culture. I took no fee from the couple, for they had contacted me out of a genuine sense of hospitality.

← A winery guesthouse
Sketch of a stone guesthouse →

ERHAUS-LONGEN
05 11 13 01

JW MARRIOTT / VENICE, 2015

Day after day, tourists queue outside the Doge's Palace in Venice. The crowds rightly want to see the monumental building that symbolises Venice's power. The most important room of the palace used to host the Doge's private office. On one side, it overlooks St. Mark's Square, and on the other, the island of San Giorgio and the Grand Canal with its bustle of boats. This room is now the seat of Venice's Cultural Heritage Department, and it is no wonder this powerful authority is located here: it is the be-all and end-all of Venice's administration.

The Heritage Department categorically forbids any modern construction and monitors renovations and restorations down to the last detail. If these laws were not strictly enforced, the splendour of Venice would no longer exist, and the city would have been ruined. Despite its vulnerability, Venice lives on thanks to this immense conservation effort.

We were delighted when we won the competition for the design of a new JW Marriott Resort & Spa on Isola delle Rose, a private island in the lagoon south of Venice. Not only were we proud to have won, we were determined to develop an exemplary scheme in this historic setting.

We researched the island's history and used our findings to create a concept that combined design with understated luxury. We presented the scheme to the Wiesbaden investor, who was pleased with the result but warned us, «Now comes the moment of truth, you must sell it to the Heritage office.» Knowing that no new buildings would be allowed, we planned to preserve the 19 abandoned buildings on the island by «filling» them with new functions. One of my colleagues had a simple idea: to build new walls inside the historic buildings, about a metre away from the original facades, which would all be restored. This «nesting» system allowed us to create new hotel rooms, a spa, a gym, restaurants, and all the amenities required for the resort.

I had a sleepless night before the appointment. The meeting would make or break the project. I was shaking nervously as I walked into the former office of the Doge. As I started to explain our vision to the Head of the Heritage department, she stopped me short with a movement of her hand, which I interpreted as «Don't say another word, it's a no.» Instead, she studied the general plan for a few minutes and said: «Mr. Thun, how can I help you?» **What a relief. She had understood that we understood Venice. I was very moved.**

Had she rejected our idea, it would not just have led to the demise of the project but also spelled the end for the Isola delle Rose. She also recognised that a project management overseen by Americans and financed by German capital, along with an Italian understanding of the essence of the location, would guarantee the project's success.

The island has been transformed into a family-friendly five-star resort with 266 rooms and a spa, steeped in nature and history, anchored in the present, and setting new benchmarks for the future of tourism.

JW Marriott Venice Resort & Spa →
View from the rooftop of the JW Marriott in Venice →

JW MARRIOTT

SANTA MARIA A CETRELLA / CAPRI, 2001–2023

Capri is somewhat pejoratively called *lo scoglio* by the residents of the island of Ischia, the second shining pearl in the Gulf of Naples. For us, «the rock» represents twenty-two unforgettable years. The happy moments that we had as a family on Capri can neither be counted nor put into words that would do them justice.

I often climbed up the Grotta Bianca with the children, and we all plunged in the sea from whatever height each of us found acceptable. Leopold often dared to jump the full thirty metres, but always waited until he could impress a passing boat of American tourists, who would enthusiastically photograph and film him. He hoped to earn a euro per tourist with his performance but all he ever received was admiration.

Guests visiting us for the first time were subjected by Leopold and Constantin to an aptitude test before the *aperitivo*. It consisted in making them climb the rock behind our house, in their simple poolside attire. Only after this would the rascals clear the way and leave us to enjoy a long evening.

Sometimes I set off before sunrise for the *Passetiello*, the oldest link between Capri and Anacapri. The steep climb is well worth it: the sunrise to the east over the mountains of Positano is magnificent and the panoramic view of the mainland and the Galli Islands is breathtaking. At the top lies the church of Santa Maria a Cetrella. It was once occupied by a hermit, who lived there for decades before it was taken over by some young people so they could party undisturbed. Our Parson Jack Russell accompanied me once on my early morning escapade but, **by the time the sun had risen, the dog was nowhere to be seen.** I went looking for him in the chapel and there he was, seated comfortably on the elevated altar, basking in the sunlight, and entranced by the sound of Pink Floyd. This place between heaven and earth was immortalised in verses by Rainer Maria Rilke. The poet also fell under the spell of the island and spent several summers on Capri.

← Santa Maria a Cetrella and Toni

MANUS FACTOR / BÜRGENSTOCK, 2010–2023

The exclusive Bürgenstock Resort was once considered the St. Tropez of the Swiss Alps. This is where, in the 1950s and 1960s, Audrey Hepburn, Sophia Loren and other film stars chose to hold their weddings, and where the German Chancellor Adenauer conducted state affairs in the summer. Those golden days were over, and a major renovation was underway when, in 2010 Qatari investors acquired the Waldhotel.

The Bürgenstock mountain is a semi-peninsula jutting into Lake Lucerne. The resort's hotels all had views both of the lake to the north and of the meadows and forests of the Italian Alps to the south. The Waldhotel was the exception and faced only south.

The hotel was to be completely redesigned as Europe's first health hotel, a Health & Wellbeing hospitality venue twinned with Nidwalden's hospital care services. It was then that I realised the scale of the demand for this new hospitality model and was persuaded to build a twelve-storey building, which we were going to gently integrate into the flank of the mountain and the surrounding landscape.

This project gave us the opportunity to design every single aspect of it, from the architecture and the interiors to the product design for the styling. For the latter we set up our company Manus Factor—Latin for handmade. We furnished every floor, including with own-design wallpaper, with patterns I had painted by hand in Capri. We also designed the outdoor wooden furniture, and our lighting designs were entrusted to a Milan manufacturer.

The all-round design exercise gave way to an amazing holistic concept, although perhaps this level of detail was lost on the Middle East investors, who took note of it but were mainly concerned with obtaining a five-star establishment specialising in healthcare.

This last aspect of the project has been an eye-opener, and I have since embraced the idea of infusing health into hospitality and hospitality into healthcare. This led me to coin the term «hospitecture.» *Hospes* means host in Latin, which shows just how intimately entwined healthcare and hospitality are. This project on the Bürgenstock allowed us to take our first tentative steps in this direction, which I hoped would shape a new holistic future for health.

Waldhotel Health & Medical Excellence, Bürgenstock →

THE FOREST CLINIC / EISENBERG, 2017–2020

In 2017 we entered a European competition to design a public hospital facility in Eisenberg, Germany. During the selection process, one of the competition managers called to inquire further about our experience in designing healthcare facilities. I readily responded, «I have never designed a hospital in my life.» He thanked me politely for my candid answer, and I presumed we would never hear from them again.

To my surprise, the opposite happened and a few months later we were announced as the winner of the competition. At that time we had completed about seventy hotel projects, so we had submitted a concept for a hospital building that put the «hospes,» the host, at the centre. We knew exactly what guests needed, how to welcome them and make them feel at home. It appears that the hospital director was open to this analogy with hospitality when planning this public hospital, which had to be built on a shoestring budget. Our expertise was exactly what he needed.

Our previous experience in «hospitecture» on the Bürgenstock came to full fruition in this project in the Thuringian forest, where we were again able to apply a fully holistic concept through architecture, interiors and styling. Patients at the Waldkliniken, which specialises in orthopaedics, experience a sense of peace and security in their hospital environment. The circular building, clad in local wood, offers spacious shared verandas connecting the rooms, all of which open onto the surrounding natural greenery. The entrance area welcomes guests with an open fireplace and each floor features a different colour scheme. Importantly, food is part of the cure, and the three restaurants are open to external guests wishing to enjoy a quality meal.

This innovative healthcare model has won numerous awards and has been shown to help patients recover more quickly—an aspect that is attracting an increasing interest from insurance companies in Germany.

← The circular building Waldkliniken Eisenberg

«Through the sustainable production of cosmetics, we encourage people to care not only for themselves, but also for the environment in which they live and work, and for the things that are important to them.» The ideology of family-owned haircare brand Davines struck a chord with our own values.

The holistic approach of the Italian natural cosmetics company was to be reflected in their new headquarters, which would include production facilities as well as administrative offices. We were able to win the selection process relatively easily thanks to our clear intent, in line with our conscious design approach, to maximise the wellbeing of their staff while minimising any impact on the environment.

We visualised a small village, with cottages housing the company's administrative offices. These are surrounded by gardens, conceived with the assistance of a local landscape and garden designer, and featuring the plants that the cosmetics company uses in its products. The canteen is a lively gathering space modelled on a greenhouse. Finally, the production facilities have been concealed so that from the nearby Milan-Bologna motorway all that is visible is a green mound of excavated material.

The opening ceremony in Parma was not attended by any eminent Italian politician, but by Bhutan's young Minister for Happiness. That's right, Bhutan has a member of the government in charge of Gross National Happiness instead of Gross Domestic Product. Following the speech of the heavily pregnant company representative, one of their employees addressed the gathering: **He felt like he was coming home to «Davine's village.» The very idea of work had been turned on its head.** He no longer saw his work as work, but simply enjoyed what he was doing. **This has been one of the nicest compliments I have ever received as an architect.**

An office environment in harmony with nature →

The island of Murano, the mecca of Venetian glassblowing, is very close to my heart and I am delighted to be working on giving it a new lease of life with a new hotel that embraces its heritage and transforms and enriches its tradition with contemporary flair.

The Langham Venice will be established in an exceptional site which includes a former glass factory and the 16th century Casino Mocenigo, with its stunning frescoes by pupils of Renaissance painter Paolo Veronese. The luxury resort will be accessed directly from the lagoon, and feature a lush garden at its heart that will offer travellers from around the world the sense of tranquillity that one seeks in a retreat.

We began working on the project in 2019 a year before the pandemic hit and slowed us down. Our proposals for the 138 rooms and suites had to be approved remotely by the Hong Kong investor and operator, and we did not meet again in person until 2023 when they were at last free again to travel to Milan.

During lockdown came the need for urgent advice from the Venice Heritage Office, but it was of course closed. The Heritage Superintendent, who had replaced the one we had met while working on the Isola delle Rose resort, agreed to come to the site despite the restrictions. We had to keep our distance, but she inspected the site in detail and listed all her requirements for preserving its historic status. Her name was Rosi, and she appeared to be won over by our ideas. Following our visit, she went above and beyond her duty, advising us personally over a period of two years.

Rosi was unexpectedly unable to attend our conclusive meeting in Murano, which would seal the approval for the project. «Send me the plans, I'll check everything,» she instructed me on the phone. We put together a parcel weighing over twenty kilos and sent it to her home on the Lido. When the deadline for an answer was reached, I phoned her full of apprehension: Venice had recently been severely hit in the flood of the century, during which the lagoon water had risen by 1.85 metres above sea level. We had made provisions in the project to protect the site against such extreme events by raising the structures by 1.5 metres. It wasn't technically legal, but that's what was on the plans we submitted. «Have you been through the documents? What do you think?» I asked Rosi nervously. «I never opened the box. It's in the entrance exactly as it arrived, but you have my OK, you can start,» was her surprisingly honest answer.

The happy ending will hopefully arrive in 2026 with the opening of the resort. Our experience on Murano has shown that even bureaucracy is made up of people, and that people are human.

← The Langham Venice, Murano

LE ZATTERE / VENICE, 2019

Venice is one of those rare places where it is pleasant to get lost, wandering through the winding alleys formed by its ancient buildings on stilts, accompanied by the melody of the water lapping persistently against this man-made miracle. Venice is a total work of art that instils a sense of eternity. My wife Susanne and I fell in love with the city and set out to make it our home.

We had our eyes on a house opposite the Peggy Guggenheim Museum on the Grand Canal but during one of our visits, Susanne opened a window onto a side canal and the smell pouring in was so nauseating that it made us reconsider its purchase and we decided to take more time to reach a decision. We were in the square in front of the palazzo when a surveyor contacted me: «Come to Le Zattere, there might be something here for you.»

Le Zattere is an area of the Dorsoduro district. The «hard ridge» is the only area of Venice built on dry land. Curious about this new-found opportunity, we made the ten-minute walk to Le Zattere. We were greeted by the owner of a neo-Gothic building built in 1906: «My wife died a week ago and coming to this house makes me feel so sad that I have decided to sell,» the grieving octogenarian told us. The house is beautifully located in the south of Dorsoduro. **Nine of its twenty-six windows overlook the Canale della Giudecca, it has a large terrace and, thanks to its solid foundations, there was not a single crack in the walls.** We agreed to buy on the spot.

Now Susanne's mission was to complete the renovation of the property and have it fully furnished within six months in time for the Biennale, when our son Leopold would arrive with a Lithuanian artist he was promoting and who was exhibiting his work at the Biennale.

This time we left the Heritage office out of the equation, completely sealed off the building and did what had to be done behind closed doors. We converted three rooms into one large living space, restored the terrazzo floors and had a long table built in the dining room to comfortably seat up to fourteen people.

Susanne's dedication rewarded us with the mix of styles that characterises the residences we are privileged to call home, where she naturally associates opposites by combining personal treasures, design objects and furniture rarities. Everything was ready by May, for the opening of the 2019 Biennale, and the inauguration of our home in the company of guests from the art and cultural scene, including the aforementioned Augustus Serapinas, the youngest artist to exhibit at the 58th Venice Biennale.

View on the Canale della Giudecca →

CUNY

CONSTANTIN AND LEOPOLD / NEW YORK, BERLIN, LONDON, 2023

My sons are at home in the art world: Constantin is an artist who divides his time between Berlin and New York, and Leopold runs his own art gallery in London. They are completely immersed in art.

The same goes for me, although as an architect I am a service provider, not a building artist. This distinction has always seemed essential to me, because when you are serving a client and a cause your ego should have no relevance, you must focus on eco, which encompasses ecology and economy. This should not be a mere promise, it should be accompanied by a credible strategy aimed at performing a service, not a solo concert. I believe this is the spirit that animated Renaissance master builders such as Brunelleschi and Palladio, who above all ensured that a building could be used sensibly and would last.

I have nevertheless encouraged the creativity of my sons, just as my parents did with me. From the age of four, every other year I was taken to the Venice Art Biennale. As a boy, these trips seemed rather annoying and uninteresting, but they instilled in me, just as it did with my boys, a deep love of art and a genuine belief in the value it brings to society.

Leopold has an obvious entrepreneurial streak and is fascinated by risk. He runs his gallery with dedication, finding and promoting emerging artists. Constantin has probably taken the most honourable, long and difficult path as an individual gone in search of himself. As an independent artist, his only limits are his own. He is a visual artist who, when asked whether he is a painter, a sculptor, a photographer, or an installation artist, would never give a complete answer.

They both have qualities that make me very proud. I am also very proud of their decision not to follow in my footsteps and be content with a nice, comfortable place in their father's business.

← Constantin and Leopold at the start of the Children's Race in 1996

FRATELLI TUTTI

Matteo Thun has designed two installations dedicated to Jose Bergoglio, inspired by the current Pope's Encyclica «Fratelli tutti.» One in the Alps that is made in wood and another in the Tuscan Apennines made in stone.

The installations aim to highlight the soul of the places and to encourage everyone to find themselves. To initiate conversations that are open to all. To foster connection, understanding and trust between people of different cultures and religions.

They are an invitation to observe the Earth in dialogue with nature and the universe, which man shares with other species and other planets.

«There is reason, after all, that some people wish to colonize the moon, and others dance before it as an ancient friend.» (James Baldwin)

«In the midst of beings as a whole an open place occurs. There is a clearing, a lighting... Only this clearing grants to us humans a passage to those beings that we ourselves are not, and access to the being that we ourselves are.» (Martin Heidegger)

ENCYCLICA

Come un fratello o una sorella
Ospitalità
Silenzio e ascolto
Dialogo
La vita è l'arte dell'incontro
Avviare processi d'incontro
Esercitare la gentilezza
Sogniamo come un'unica umanità
"Gli altri" sono i "noi"
Consapevolezza di umanità
Uguaglianza
Solidarietà
Senza escludere nessuno
(g. Montini)
Verso lo sviluppo solidale
di tutti i popoli
Autenticità
Ammirare le bellezze del mondo
Una nuova sintesi
Solidarietà e reciprocità

Jorge Mario Bergoglio

← A contemplative wooden installation in the Alps
A contemplative stone installation →

SUSANNE THUN

When we became a couple forty-two years ago, Matteo began buying me large bouquets of red roses. These romantic gifts became even more intense when, in a second phase, each bouquet was accompanied by a note in Post-it form which often included a drawing. After marriage came the *Sturm und Drang* period, which meant that I only received heartfelt drawings with my flowers.

He would buy me flowers when he passed a flower shop on his way home from work and picked one of the last, lonely and somewhat sad stems that were left, usually on a Friday evening when flowers are no longer as fresh as dew. The beauty of these bouquets lay in the heartfelt intention behind the gifts. I have kept every single Post-it, every single card, every single message safely stored in cardboard boxes, they form my precious collection of «Love letters from Matteo.»

When we bought our house in Capri, I took on the challenge of designing the garden. With the help of the gardener, I studied the entire Mediterranean flora and put my heart and soul into it. My pride and joy was an old hibiscus that we had carefully nurtured to finally produce a flower.

Anticipating the arrival of friends, I dedicated an entire week on the island to meticulously prepare everything for Matteo and our guests. When he arrived, he wandered into the garden and cut the hibiscus flower I had spent days worshipping, which I found in a vase on the table—what a disaster! This was one of his favourite hobbies, to put all sorts of vases around the house and fill them with fresh flowers from the garden. On that occasion I have had to put my foot down: «Matteo, you don't touch the flowers in the garden!» We had all sorts of beautiful specimens in our garden, from English roses to lemon trees, but from that day forth he has had to venture in the neighbour's garden to cut any flowers.

Nowadays, Matteo surprises me with bouquets of wildflowers he gathers during his walks in the Engadine. The nice thing about them is not only that he thinks of me during his walks and that he wants to make me happy, meadow flowers are actually my favourite.

It began with opulent romantic red roses, and as life evolved through various stages, the flowers I continue to receive from Matteo remain my cherished and delightful sign of affection.

← Susanne and Matteo on their bikes in Milan
Susanne and Matteo →

MATTHIAS BRUNNER

Most people are familiar with this situation: You are a guest in a foreign setting and you walk into a room full of faces you have never seen before. If you're lucky, you meet two pairs of eyes that greet you with curiosity. This is what happened with Matteo and Susanne Thun when I first met them in S-Chanf, in company of art-loving friends in a crowded «Stüva» for a simple dinner of boiled potatoes with bacon and cheese. Both were disarmingly charming and warm, so meeting them was an instant pleasure. After we had exchanged a few words, I knew—or rather hoped—that we would become friends.

Film Director Douglas Sirk, a master in the production of Hollywood melodramas starring Lana Turner and Rock Hudson, stood next to me and in a fatherly tone explained why the best training for a director was not a film degree but an education in architecture. This has been confirmed to me time and time again by other directors. If only because of the lighting. You don't need to remember Fritz Lang's «*Metropolis*» to understand this. I took good note of his observation and later visited Frank Loyd Wright's houses with Paul Morrissey and Andy Warhol. What a school of vision! The love for good architecture has stayed with me ever since. Like Matteo and Susanne, I love great cinema and when you talk to them and see their homes, you know that they have studied their role models closely. Nothing is left to chance. No «flavour of the day!»

In Matteo's case, however, this consideration also works the other way round, thanks to his extensive knowledge of the classics of film history, especially Italian cinema and the films of Antonioni in particular. In this way, Matteo witnessed on screen what kind of architecture we need to live a happy life, and where architecture can become too dominant and make life difficult for us. The same is true when a client's elegance knows no bounds and the architecture can easily fall into this trap. In these cases, Matteo's curiosity about people and their environment helps him to master this balance with confidence and resist the temptation of decoration.

For him, it's not about «beautiful living» and desperately marking projects with his «signature stamp,» but about tailor-made visionary architecture that should make his clients happy in the best possible way and for the long term. That's why, for him, work only begins after the most careful research into a place and its entire environment. Matteo knows that this is the only way he can lead his architecture sustainably into the future. His design for the «Vigilius Mountain Resort» is a good example of this. It follows the contours of the nearby mountains and reinterprets the traditional, local way of building.

I can hardly wait for more pilgrimages to Matteo's houses in the future. What could be better than a friendship founded on architecture, films, and our affection for our dogs, Toni and Louffy! And not even need to envisage staying at a Four Seasons Hotel. Paradise now!

Matthias Brunner, Zurich, November 2023

MARTINO GAMPER

Ceramics and design

At the time, Matteo was probably the youngest professor in Vienna, teaching at the Angewandte master class for ceramics and glass design. The year was 1984.

Matteo was something of a design evangelist. Once a month he travelled from Milan to Vienna to teach. All the students, there were only four of us in the class, looked forward to these special days with the maestro. There was a distinct feeling that a piece of Milan was always with him, which was evident in his sophisticated Milanese fashion, which was so very different from the bourgeois style of Vienna. He wore very stylish and well-tailored suits with the finest cashmere turtlenecks in winter and silk shirts in summer. Our class was very diverse: some were budding designers who saw their future in craftsmanship and small-scale production, others wanted to bring new products to market, influenced by the zeitgeist around Alessi, Philippe Starck, Giulio Cappellini.

While teaching, Matteo shared with us his invaluable experience of the industry and the various manufacturing processes. He was keen to guide young designers to find their own way into the industry and learn to navigate the market.

Fast forward: Drawing and writing

When I moved from Vienna to Milan in the summer of 1996 to work as an industrial designer in Matteo Thun's studio in Via Appiani, one thing became clear to me: Milan was the complete opposite of Vienna, the architecture, the food, the style.

At Matteo's *Arti & Mestieri* we were a diverse group of designers, architects and graphic artists working both on small products and on larger projects. I remember the client meetings and presentations that took place in a very bright, elegant meeting room on the first floor.

Matteo was «capo tavola» and we young designers sat on the side. Matteo's speciality was to draw freehand in front of the client with his left hand, while at the same time taking notes with his right hand—incredible! When I saw this for the first time, it became clear to me that Matteo was a jack-of-all-trades—omnidextrous and omnifarious.

Those moment spent observing these presentations were the best school for us newcomers. It was about actual industrial design with real and important clients, discussing very clearly and openly design, production and contractual agreements. I greatly admired this professional, respectful, and transparent way of dealing with people, I have retained these values and still apply this model in my own studio today.

Clear language leads to long-lasting friendships.

Martino Gamper, London, November 2023

OLIVER JAHN

In 1984 the Italian writer Italo Calvino was invited by Harvard University to give the Charles Eliot Norton Poetry Lectures. Calvino had managed to finish preparing five of the six lectures, when he died shortly before he was due to leave for the United States. Hence the title «*Lezioni americane.*» «His «*Six proposals for the next millennium*» became his philosophical legacy, but also a very concrete vade mecum of artistic and creative virtues that the poet advocated: lightness, speed, accuracy, vividness, complexity and consistency.

It may have been one of those inscrutable twists of fate (that like to disguise themselves as coincidences) that led the young architect Matteo Thun to open his first office in the centre of Milan in 1984. A man with a past, one might say, because as a collaborator of the father of design, Ettore Sottsass, and co-founder of the Memphis Group, he had caused nothing less than a revolution in the overly dusty, functionalist design scene. The joyful break with all the traditions and unwritten laws of design, the play with his own creative imagination, the experimentation, the exuberant dance with form and material, suited Matteo's nature infinitely better than all the constraints of an «immobile» industry.

No wonder Matteo came across Italo Calvino's breviary. It almost sounds as if Calvino was thinking of the Milanese revolutionary when he wrote: «I have tried to remove weight, sometimes from people, sometimes from heavenly bodies, sometimes from cities; above all I have tried to remove weight from the structure of stories and from language.»

Today, when I look at the work Matteo Thun has produced over the last four decades, spread all over the world, this credo of Calvino's—taking away weight—seems to be one of the central motivations of his work. Perhaps we are even on the trail of the creative ember of a designer who, for me, has always been a philosopher: A laughing philosopher in the way of the famous pre-Socratic philosopher Democritus, whose amused light-footed approach to architecture, nature and human needs is able to leave all heaviness behind with almost programmatic consistency, without ever losing the grounding of masterful craftsmanship.

We are dealing here with the sparkling paradox of a profoundly earthy lightness that does not leave conventions, habits of thought and market expectations behind for the sake of provocation, but knows how to connect man, buildings and nature, beauty, genius loci, and materiality with a precise eye and a light hand, at once joyful and saturated with experience.

It is entirely in this spirit that Matteo Thun has spent a lifetime developing a language of design, architecture and materiality that recognises its social function and consistently and warmly places itself at the forefront of a movement. Only those who know how to take the excess weight out of things can give them the radiance of important culture that seems so easy and natural, yet is so difficult to achieve.

Oliver Jahn, Munich, November 2023

ROLF SACHS

Matteo,

Susanne
Ästhet
Modest
Observant
Wood and natural tactility
Très sporty
Humor, Witz und Schalk
Finessed
Obviously Memphis
Engadin, Amalfi coast, Venice, Milano
Stylish and fashionable
Acciughe and olives
Tintin and Poldi
Snow and sea water
Comme des garçons meets Loro Piana
Formel 1—no car
Sleepless nights
Nervenkitzel
Hiking promenades
Lausbub
Cautious risk taker
Alps and Med
Paper, paper, paper and colour pencils
Curious and resolved
Chosen wise words
Enthused and inspiring
Love
In Freundschaft

Rolf Sachs, Rome, November 2023

Sherin Kneifl is an experienced editor who has worked for renowned publications such as BUNTE, ELLE, InStyle and Süddeutsche, as well as the Swiss lifestyle and fashion magazines Style and Bolero. Her degree in psychology has shaped her empathetic writing style, as seen in her bestselling biographies of football legend Köbi Kuhn and ice hockey star Mark Streit. After completing a doctorate in law, she now pursues a successful career as a freelance journalist and author based in Zurich.

72 STORIES / CELERINA, MILAN, ZURICH, 2023

How do you put a life into words, including a career that spans half a century and produced works that are present on every continent? The best way is by telling stories, and there are a countless number of them, some private, some amusing, others touching, sad, exciting, and inspiring.

I was delighted when Matteo suggested that we put down on paper a series of intuitively chosen stories, but as an author I had to highlight the value of his work without neglecting personal moments and interpersonal relationships.

The book grew and blossomed organically over the course of a year, and from the outset the architect and designer was clear about the form in which the narrative had to be presented: all the important aspects had to be communicated through key images.

Matteo made it easy for both of us to realise his idea. I was allowed to look behind the scenes, he showed me his residences and his Milan practice, where we had long conversations during which he described and showed me what was important to him. «I want to tell what no one knows and arouses curiosity. My two sons, Constantin and Leopold, always wanted to hear stories when they were little. As there is no separation between my work and my private life, it would be nice to include both,» he explained.

This mix of private and public anecdotes makes the reader want to know more—at least that was our intention. What I will take with me from writing this book are not only the warm moments I spent in the hospitable company of Susanne and Matteo, but above all the confirmation that it is legitimate to have fun and that this could even be the driving force behind creation. Also, that humanity always comes first, that the «impossible» is what makes innovation possible, and that style is an attitude. And that a creative mind sometimes gets the best ideas while walking the dog.

by Sherin Kneifl

In 72 stories that trace the life of the Milanese architect and designer from South Tyrol, Matteo Thun talks about himself, his architecture, his designs, his values, and his beliefs.

Curiosity is the eternal driving force and the common thread of his work, which weaves together innovation, disruption, and sustainability. But who is the man behind the work? This «diary» offers a rare glimpse behind the scenes, through a wealth of professional and personal anecdotes that provide valuable insights into his career and a better understanding of the man he is. This creative biography encourages readers to find their «creative inner child.» «You just have to want it» is Matteo Thun's motto—make it yours too!

ACKNOWLEDGMENTS

I am very grateful to my wife Susanne for inspiring me to make this book and for her ever-loving support - also now for this project.

I would also like to thank the super designers I have the privilege of working with every day in the office, without whom many of the achievements described in these stories would not have been possible.

A special thank you to Marcella Prior-Callwey and Raffaela Roos for their confidence in this book.

Many thanks to Michela Brolese for the graphic layout, Cristina Lovati for coordinating the image data, and to Micaela Benini for the English translation.

I am grateful to Matthias Brunner, Martino Gamper, Oliver Jahn, and Rolf Sachs for their thoughtful insights about me.

Thank you Sherin Kneifl for the subtle storytelling.

PHOTO CREDITS

Cover: Lewis Ronald

Collage: Archive Matteo Thun

Archive Matteo Thun
p.8/9, p.10, p.12, p.13, p.15, p.19, p.20, p.23, p.24, p.27, p.28, p.32, p.35, p.36/37, p.39, p.40, p.41, p.43, p.44, p.46/47, p.50/51, p.54, p.57, p.58, p.64/65, p.69, p.70/71, p.72, p.77, p.83, p.84, p.86, p.91, p.94, p.97, p.98/99, p.102, p.106, p.112, p.114, p.117, p.118, p.122, p.125, p.126, p.136, p.143, p.146/147, p.152, p.160, p.164, p.166, p.168/169, p.170

No credit / free
p.16, p.31, p.66, p.88, p.109

Getty Images
p. 23, p.53

Archivio Natalini
p. 31

Memphis
p. 48

Studio Azzurro
p. 60/61

Andrea Martiradonna
p.63

Walter Pfeiffer
p. 74/75, p.87, p.135, p.139

illy
p. 78, p.80/81

Griffner Haus AG
p. 92/93

Olaf Gollner
p. 100

Vigilius Mountain Resort
p. 104/105

Santi Caleca
p. 121

Klaus Frahm
p.110, p.129, p.130/131

Jens Weber
p. 132

Marco Bertolini
p. 140

Linda Blatzek
p. 144

JW Marriott Venice Resort and Spa – Isola Delle Rose
p. 155

Andrea Garuti
p. 149, p.150/151

Gionata Xerra
p. 156

Max Zambelli
p. 159

photo Andrea Ferrari – production Francesca Benedetto / Courtesy Elle Decor Italia
p. 163

Fabrizio Ferri
p.172/173

Collage: Archive Matteo Thun, Daniel Chardon

CALLWEY
SEIT 1884

Klenzestraße 36
80469 München
buch@callwey.de
Tel.: +49 89 8905080-0
www.callwey.de

Find us on Instagram:
www.instagram.com/callwey

ISBN: 978-3-7667-2717-6
1st edition 2024

Bibliographic information from the German National Library:
The German National Library lists this publication in the German National Bibliography; detailed bibliographic data can be accessed on the Internet at http://dnb.d-nb.de.

This book was produced in Callwey quality for you:
For the content paper, we chose a Munken White 115 g/m2 - a high-quality natural paper that gives the content a particularly noble character. The hardcover design consists of Duchesse linen and was refined with blind embossing as well as a title label and additionally with white hot foil stamping. This book was printed and bound in Germany by optimal Media, Röbel/Müritz.

The following people hope that you will enjoy this book:

Project management
Raffaela Roos

Proofreading
Judith Marnet

Design & Typesetting
Studio Matteo Thun

Production
Oliver Meier and Stephanie Thurmair

Please notice:
It is important to us that all genders feel recognised and valued. However, in order to improve the readability of the texts, we refrain from using male, female anddiverse (m/f/d). Where possible, we endeavour to include all forms or to use neutral formulations. All personal designations apply equally to all genders. We were granted permission to photograph the works of art shown in the book on the premises of the protagonists by the protagonists themselves.

Notices shall be sent to:
Matteo Thun & Partners
Via Andrea Appiani 9
20121 Milan, Italy
info@matteothun.com

Liebevoll begleitet von
R. Roos

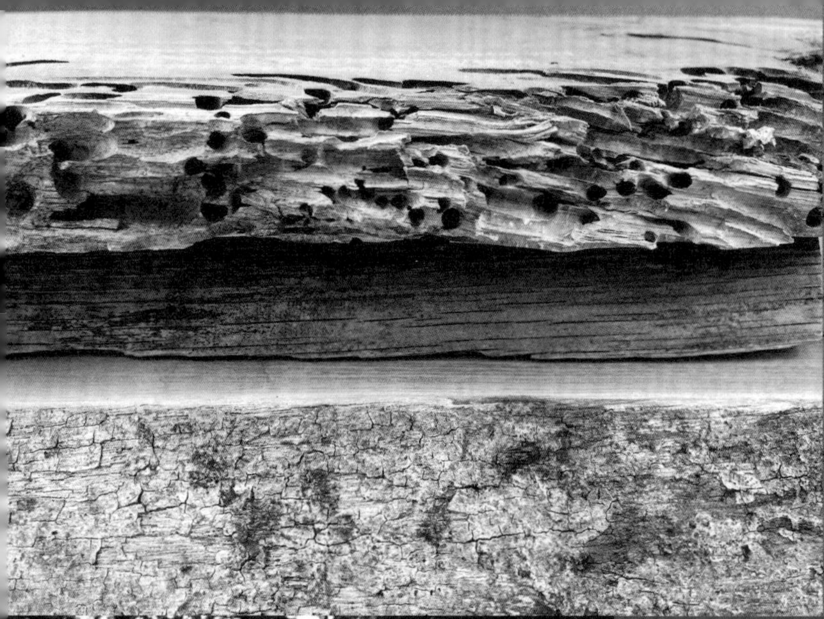